Angels
By The Roadside

A Memoir

Dora S. Gonzalez

Copyright © 2015 Dora S. Gonzalez.

All rights reserved. No part of this book may be used or reproduced by any means, graphic, electronic, or mechanical, including photocopying, recording, taping or by any information storage retrieval system without the written permission of the author except in the case of brief quotations embodied in critical articles and reviews.

This book is a work of non-fiction. Unless otherwise noted, the author and the publisher make no explicit guarantees as to the accuracy of the information contained in this book and in some cases, names of people and places have been altered to protect their privacy.

Scripture taken from the Holy Bible, NEW INTERNATIONAL VERSION®. Copyright © 1973, 1978, 1984 by Biblica, Inc. All rights reserved worldwide. Used by permission. NEW INTERNATIONAL VERSION® and NIV® are registered trademarks of Biblica, Inc. Use of either trademark for the offering of goods or services requires the prior written consent of Biblica US, Inc.

WestBow Press books may be ordered through booksellers or by contacting:

WestBow Press
A Division of Thomas Nelson & Zondervan
1663 Liberty Drive
Bloomington, IN 47403
www.westbowpress.com
1 (866) 928-1240

Because of the dynamic nature of the Internet, any web addresses or links contained in this book may have changed since publication and may no longer be valid. The views expressed in this work are solely those of the author and do not necessarily reflect the views of the publisher, and the publisher hereby disclaims any responsibility for them.

Any people depicted in stock imagery provided by Thinkstock are models, and such images are being used for illustrative purposes only. Certain stock imagery © Thinkstock.

ISBN: 978-1-5127-1746-4 (sc)
ISBN: 978-1-5127-1747-1 (hc)
ISBN: 978-1-5127-1745-7 (e)

Library of Congress Control Number: 2015917534

Print information available on the last page.

WestBow Press rev. date: 11/12/2015

CONTENTS

Dedication vii
Introduction 1

Chapter 1   Angels by the Literal Roadside 3
            An Angel in a Hot Rod 6
            Angels in Las Vegas? 8

Chapter 2   Folktales and Angels 10
            Children Experience God Too............................11
            Growing Up to Greater Experiences.....................14
            A Teenager in Love..16

Chapter 3   No College on the Horizon................................ 20
            Sun Rays at Last 21
            God's New Plans Revealed 26

Chapter 4   A Missionary at Last......................................29
            A Mighty Rushing Wind..................................36
            College Bound 38

Chapter 5   Angels Explain God's "No"............................... 43

Chapter 6   Wedding Bells..49

Chapter 7	Me, a Pastor?	58
	A Spiritual Shift	61
	A New Revelation	64
Chapter 8	Healing Wings	68
	Leave Ebenezer?	72
Chapter 9	A Dark Cloud	78
	Swords of Fire	80
	Angels to the Rescue	83
	A New Opened Door	84
Chapter 10	Moving Forward	89
Chapter 11	The Gates of Hell Break Loose	94
Chapter 12	Angels Will Welcome Me Home	98

DEDICATION

I dedicate this book to my faithful companion, my Lord and Savior, Jesus Christ. He made my life worth living. He has been there all the time, never leaving or forsaking me in life's journey. The experiences I share in this book could never have happened without Him, and I could never have endured or lived to tell about them without His help. How I love my Jesus.

I also dedicate this book in memory of my beloved *angel*, the very special vessel God used to bring me into this world: my mom, Carmen Caraveo. Just as Jacob in the Bible could see a special calling upon the life of his son Joseph, Mom knew God had chosen me to be the stronghold of the family. She declared it even in her last wish when the time came for her to appoint an executrix in her will. Only she, with divine guidance, knew why she picked me out of her nine children to manage her estate. Was it because she had walked with me throughout my ministry? Whatever the reason, she was my right hand in every endeavor, my faithful supporter, and my strongest prayer warrior. I learned that there is truly no sweeter title than Mother, Mom, or "Amá," as we all called her.

I also dedicate this memoir to my loving husband, Reynaldo R. González, my daughter, Dina Ann, and my sons, Reynaldo (Rey Jr.) and Miguel (Mike) González. It is because of them and the special role each has played in my life that I was inspired to write this book and leave with them the vivid experiences of my life. My goal is that my family and subsequent generations may come to know Jesus and confide in Him as I have—that they may trust that what He has done for me, He will do for them also.

My world would have been so small and void if I would have been the only child in the Silva family. It is with great respect and love that I also dedicate this book in memory of my dad, Miguel Silva, and to each one of my siblings. From eldest to youngest, they are Carmen, Hilda, Ayola, Aureliano, Miguel, Arnulfo, Anita, and Melva. Nine of us surrounded Mom and Dad in their everyday lives, and all nine of us plan to see them again in our heavenly home someday. What a joy that will be.

Last but not least, I dedicate this work to my faithful friends and the loyal members of Templo Ebenezer Assembly of God Church in San Benito, Texas. I thank them for their love, support, and patience. I thank them for being there for us, their pastoral family, during these thirty years of my pastorate, and for witnessing the glacial pace at which this book was completed and published.

My mother, Carmen Caraveo Silva (1915–1995).

My siblings and me, in descending order by age, from left to right: Carmen, me, Hilda, Ayola, Aureliano, Miguel, Arnulfo, Anita, and Melva; photograph taken in 2007.

INTRODUCTION

My life has always been church centered. And because I have shared so many of my experiences with the congregation of the two churches I have pastored in the last thirty-five years, I decided to write *Angels by the Roadside* to consolidate my stories, visions, dreams, revelations, and angelic visitations in one place.

When teaching or preaching on a weekly basis, I occasionally insert into a lesson or a sermon one of those encounters I have had with real angels. No, none ever had wings. None ever spoke with a thunderous voice surrounded by a bright light. Instead, those angels always took the form of humans and then inexplicably vanished.

Of course, my children (Dina, Rey, and Mike) know most, if not all, of the stories by heart. My husband, because of his illness, rejoices but cannot retain a story for more than a few minutes, because multiple sclerosis has affected the memory centers of his brain. While I cannot share with him all the stories and blessings the Lord and I have experienced, Dina and the boys make up for the loss. They not only have heard my stories but also have been eyewitnesses in one place or another and in different situations where no one else could have helped me but the Lord Himself through His heavenly agents.

My experiences with the angelic were so known to my family that once Dina looked at me as if seeing a ghost and asked, "What did God tell you?" I smiled and nodded. I wanted her to see God in me to the extent that she would desire the same for her life.

Rey's faith solidified as he grew. His faith in God and His supernatural power became unwavering, as it remains to this day. He has reminded me that God's angels could very well be standing next to me, encouraging me to be brave when the burden seems too heavy to carry or when I feel alone. He's reminded me of this occasion or that when God has sent His angelic hosts my way. This showed me that my work had not been in vain. He too has come to believe in God's heavenly messengers and has dedicated time in reading and learning about them. The topic has become one of such interest to him that he has even shared with his Sunday school class excerpts from Billy Graham's book titled *Angels, God's Secret Agents*. That has made me very proud and has encouraged me to continue with my long-ago set goal of writing this book, trusting that a youth from his class would read my own experiences and eventually share them with someone else too.

That Mike had treasured my stories was made obvious one day when he shared in his philosophy class one of my encounters with angels. The subject that day being metaphysics, the topic lent itself to discussions on supernatural beings. Mike took advantage of the topic to share not only what I believed but also what he himself had seen, heard, and learned about angels. He had been an eyewitness to more than one of God's celestial visitors sent to open doors or reveal His plans to me in unthinkable ways.

It is, therefore, a privilege for me to compile my diary notes, my paper clippings, and my lengthy drafts in this book with the hope that my daughter and sons will keep the proverbial torch lit in their lives and will tell even the unwritten anecdotes for generations to come.

I hope and pray that *Angels by the Roadside* will encourage your faith and reassure you of your value to God. He will make his presence known, even if it is through an envoy sent from heaven. I honor God for the experiences He's allowed me to live and for the privilege of recording them in this special work.

CHAPTER 1

Angels by the Literal Roadside

Like a slide presentation, my angelic experiences flashed through my mind as I pulled out the picture album of our family's two-week vacation in 1990.

Our trips to the hospital had been the only vacations we had ever taken. My husband, Reynaldo, had been diagnosed with multiple sclerosis, or MS. At the time, the best treatments available to us were in Houston, Texas, where by 1990, we had already been going to receive treatment for six years. Dina, the boys, and I made the best of the trips from the Rio Grande Valley in South Texas to Houston and enjoyed seeing all the buildings around the medical center, especially during the Christmas holidays—admiring the elegant decorations of each. We were long due and ready for a real vacation.

I had prayed constantly, thanking God in advance for charging angels to guide and assist me on this trip. The plan was to fly to Colorado, then to Disneyland in California, and finally to Las Vegas, with a few bus rides in between. Although God did not speak to me or promise to send angels, I had repeatedly confessed and believed that they would be there for me in a time of need. Angels would assist us with love and care, I thought, because what woman in her right mind would venture away from home with a totally disabled, wheelchair-bound husband and two young children, Rey and Mike—ages ten and eight—and for two weeks?

Our first stop was Brighton, Colorado, to visit with my husband's eldest sister and her family. Their hospitality and generosity were more than we could have asked for. The whole family took it upon itself to take turns touring us in and around the area. My sons' aunts and uncles pampered them spoiled. Rey and Mike enjoyed the snow, the mountains, the mountain goats and elk, and everything else in Colorado so much that they almost forgot that we were en route to California.

Spending time with my husband's sister, Asilia, was a blessing we still treasure. Because both were ill, Reynaldo and Asilia would embrace as if thinking they would never see each other again. I promised we would be back, and that hope gave way to a change of atmosphere at our departure. We joked and laughed about how strong they both looked—that it would not surprise us if they would outlive us all. The farewell was painful. We hugged and cried together. After issuing a prayer, we left for Disneyland.

My husband, Reynaldo R. González, seen with his sister Asilia G. Huerta; March 2001, during a subsequent visit.

Angels by the Literal Roadside

Everything had been great until we got to Anaheim, California. I needed God's help and needed it fast. The travel agent back home had assured me that our hotel would be immediately across the street from Disneyland. This was important because I needed to let my husband rest and check on him periodically while still being able to entertain the boys across the street. The airport shuttle, however, had dropped us off not across the street but at a hotel about two miles from Disneyland. There I stood, with my family and luggage, outside a dark, rundown motel with no handicap rooms and without a vehicle with which to transport ourselves. The hotel manager was alone in the office and could not help. Worse yet, the shuttle that dropped us off had already left. As I stood there trying to decide what to do, I looked up, and with tears in my eyes, hoping the boys wouldn't notice, I issued a short prayer, reminding God that I was relying on Him. He had heard me confess it time and again. I knew he saw my tears and heard my prayer, because He intervened immediately and miraculously.

As soon as I finished my quick prayer, a gentleman came out of his room and greeted us cheerfully, especially glad to know that we too were from Texas and specifically from "the Valley." He asked if we knew anyone from his hometown. I told him that I only knew a pastoral family whose last name was Vera. With the mention of that name, he literally rushed toward us and hugged us all. He happened to be one of Pastor Vera's sons who I had never met. With a huge grin, he repeated, "What a small world," but in my heart, I knew he was the *first angel* sent to assist me. When I explained the situation and why we were still standing in the parking lot, he offered to take us to the Disneyland area. He took it upon himself to check us in at the Ramada Inn across the street from the park. Later that evening, we met again at a mini golf establishment next to the hotel, which is when he stated that he and his family were leaving in the morning. To this day, I have never seen or heard from him again. Twenty-five years later, I firmly believe he was *an angel by the roadside* sent by God in the hour of need to aid me at that particular place, at that particular time.

An Angel in a Hot Rod

With each passing page of the photo album, more memories flooded my mind. After a few days of visiting Disneyland, Hollywood, and other attractions around Los Angeles, we took the bus to Santa María. It was quite a scene to see my husband climb into the bus, but with the aid of a few male passengers volunteering to help him, we managed to get settled. The bus-ride portion of our trip was in our itinerary, but more important, in God's plan to show me that, consistent with my declaration, He was ready for us to have another angelic visitation.

Our Greyhound bus broke down somewhere in the middle of nowhere and about one mile from the nearest town, with only a McDonald's and one other restaurant. The bus driver announced it would be a few hours before a replacement bus would arrive to take us the rest of the way. In the meantime, everyone else got off and headed in the direction of the eateries. I could not get my husband down and could not leave him alone either, so we stayed behind. It did not occur to me to ask someone to grab something to eat for the boys on their way back, so we would just have to wait. My heart broke when Rey and Mike begged to go to McDonald's, but when I explained why we could not go, they settled for a promise of a "special treat" when we'd get to Santa Maria.

I could not and should not cry. I had to be strong for my husband and my boys. I couldn't even pray for fear I'd burst into tears. My heart pounded so hard and loud that I feared the kids could hear it. When I finally did pray, choking with tears, I reminded God of our traveling "deal." I shook my head, took a deep breath, and bravely turned to entertain the kids. Moments later, a red convertible Corvette pulled up beside the bus. Puzzled, I asked myself, an angel in a hot rod?

One expects to see a young person in a convertible Corvette, but this was an elderly, gray-haired man in his seventies. He asked what we were doing alone by the bus. I explained to him about the disabled bus, how the driver and passengers had all gone to grab a bite, and why we couldn't go. As if he had interacted with children all his life, he lovingly stooped down to ask my boys if they were hungry. He knew the answer before they had a chance to reply and immediately offered to take us to the McDonald's down the road. The boys, fascinated with the car, were happy to climb right in, but I wasn't about to get in a sports car with a stranger. When I politely turned down his offer, he turned to me and said, "I'll be right back with some lunch for all of you." He wouldn't take any money from me, so I really doubted that he'd be back.

To my surprise, minutes later the red Corvette drove up again with a meal for each of us. The gray-haired man refused to take any money, wished us well, and took off quickly, giving the boys one last show of his car's power. With overwhelming excitement, we joined my husband inside the bus and sat to enjoy our treat. Imagine the boys' delight—first a "totally awesome" car and then the pinnacle of a growing boy's food pyramid: McDonald's! We talked about our visitor in the red hot rod for a long time until the bus driver and passengers returned, just in time to transfer to another bus.

We finally made it to Santa Maria, where some of my relatives would host us for a few days. They had been worried when we didn't arrive at the scheduled time, but after sharing our story, we all praised God for His traveling mercies. When it was time for us to move on, not for the life of them would they allow us to continue by bus. My aunt and cousins drove us to our next destination, which was a two-hour drive. Just as our relatives in Colorado had expressed, they too were amazed at the sight of me traveling with my husband, in as bad a shape as he looked, and with two energetic kids who wanted to go everywhere and see everything. They told me I was the most courageous woman they had ever seen.

After I told them about my entire life's walk with the Lord and how I relied on His companionship and promises, I think they admired my faith more than my courage. I quoted Scripture verses about how His angels went before us. In the end, I believe my aunt and cousins felt the same security I did—that God would keep us safe the remainder of our trip until we would arrive back home, safe and sound.

Angels in Las Vegas?

My last angel on this trip, Brother Isaías Olvera, was not a stranger; rather, he was a dear friend of my husband and a former Bible school student of mine. My cousins had driven us to his home in Bakersfield, California. Our visit with him and his family was one of spiritual refreshment. We shared with each other about God's blessings in our lives and caught up on happenings since our last visit in Texas.

The Olvera family took us sightseeing at the nearby Sequoia National Park and other tourist attractions. They had so many other places to take us to, but we were running out of time. Our check-in date at the Circus Circus Hotel in Las Vegas was on July 3, as our goal was to spend the Fourth celebrating our nation's independence in full color in Las Vegas with thousands of lights that promised to illuminate the night sky.

Like my relatives in Santa Maria, Brother Olvera and his wife insisted on taking us to Vegas, not allowing us to take the bus as we had previously planned. Praise God for their insistence, because I don't know what I would've done without them. As such, they would turn out be the angels God would use. They drove us to Vegas, helped us check in at the hotel, and even took us on a short tour to acquaint us with the tram that we needed to use to and from the hotel during the next few days. After spending some time checking out the casinos and making sure we were settled, they returned home. Rey and Mike had learned their way in and around the hotel just as they had been instructed by Brother Olvera. I would have been lost, had it not been for their excellent navigational skills. What an unforgettable time we had, and how I thanked God for His faithfulness in providing assistance the whole way.

We enjoyed our bus ride back to Anaheim. After spending one more day at Disneyland, we finally flew back home. While a fourteen-day vacation seemed long for me, the boys thought it short. They never complained or seemed to mind the inconveniences of transferring their dad from one vehicle to another or pushing the wheelchair in the 113-degree temperature in Vegas. They were having fun, and that was all that mattered. Dina had been to Vegas before and had decided to stay home with her aunts to help with staffing fireworks stands that her aunts ran each year during the Fourth of July sales season. Both boys came back home eager to share with Dina the new phrase they had thought of: "Vacation—the most beautiful word in the English language."

As I sat there, flipping the pages of the photo album, the experiences in California and Vegas brought to my mind memories of other angelic visitations throughout my life. My earliest memory is of a time when I was only nine years old. Although new to the faith at that age, what I had learned about angels, even then, helped me to distinguish between folktales and truly divine apparitions. God's special appearances through dreams, visions, or revelations provoked a chain of events in my life resulting in extraordinary experiences during my walk down the road of life.

CHAPTER 2

Folktales and Angels

It all seemed like a joke when a cousin would warn us about the guardian angels watching over us and how displeased they would be if we were talking while eating at the table. The topic of angels was occasionally heard during family get-togethers while the elders shared stories about the supernatural to entertain the company. I outgrew believing all kinds of tales at a very early age, whether they were fairy tales, enchanted horror folktales, or supernatural (usually evil) experiences people shared. This change came about when I had a personal encounter with God at age nine. I came to love God in such a way that I knew, even as a child, that He kept watch over His children and that He would communicate with His people through personified celestial beings called angels.

    In Sunday school, I had learned about angels who, taking the form of human beings, walked and talked to Abraham about God's plan to destroy the cities of Sodom and Gomorrah. If the Bible said that "the angel of the Lord" appeared to this or that person, I cared less about whether it happened during the Old Testament time or the New Testament time and more about the simple fact that it happened. What I embraced about angel stories was the fact that God was so great and powerful that in His desire to speak personally to one of His faithful, He had sent His angel or angels to convey a message, to defend and protect, to guide and provide, or to simply stand by someone until the person felt secure and at peace.

My faith in the existence of angels was so rooted in my life that it helped me in my growing years as I continued to serve and trust God. As a nine-year-old, I knew without a shadow of a doubt what I was doing that morning when the minister asked if anyone wanted to give their lives to Jesus and become a newborn Christian. I had stood up, walked up to the altar, repeated the pastor's prayer for my commitment, and went home from that small community Baptist church in Los Fresnos, Texas, a total new person with an experience that would last a lifetime.

My parents didn't go to church then but would send all nine of us children with our neighbors, the Macombes (pronounced "may-comes"). Little did the Macombes know but God would honor their faith and continue working in each of us until the entire Silva family, including my parents, would eventually surrender their lives to the Lord. Mr. and Mrs. Macombe would probably never have guessed that their sacrifice would be rewarded with the eventual calling into the ministry of one of us Silva kids they took to church every Sunday morning.

I often wonder what my life, and that of my family, would be if that elderly couple would not have labored for the kingdom of God. If it were not for the Macombes, I wouldn't be writing of the beautiful experiences with the Lord since my childhood, nor would I be sharing the glorious revelations, visions, and personal encounters with God and with His messengers. Their ministry in reaching the lost would live on through me and my very own ministry.

Children Experience God Too

After experiencing salvation, I had a great desire to learn more about God and His marvelous power. It was in the summer of 1953, when I became ill with appendicitis that a series of personal encounters with the Almighty began to unfold. He truly revealed Himself to me and sealed my life for Him and for His kingdom.

After my diagnosis, it was decided that my parents would take me across the Texas border to Mexico for surgery in the following weeks. A week before the surgery, Mom had gone into town and, while there, decided to buy four pairs of underwear for my younger sister and me. That was a real treat. After all, back then, our clothes were homemade from the flour sacks or from hand-me-down pieces of cloth. (Flour was purchased by the pound in sacks, or bags made of a paper/cloth like material that, after the flour was depleted, was cut and tailored as underwear.) The new undergarments were divided between Hilda and me. I was so conscious of going to the hospital in my flour-sack, homemade panties that when given the new ones, I put them back in the bag and decided to hide them for the upcoming surgery. I have always been excellent at stowing things away for later use in very inconspicuous places—too good, I'm afraid. Two days before the surgery, I looked everywhere for the little bag and its contents. It was nowhere to be found! The bag with my "necessities" had vanished. I looked desperately for the paper bag. I cried inconsolably. I even begged Hilda to lend me hers to take to the hospital, but she wouldn't budge, and for some reason, Mom would not force her to loan them to me! Carmen, the eldest of us three, volunteered to help look for my lost bag, and Ayola, who was a year younger than Hilda, offered her underwear, but they were not new. I was at a loss.

I remember kneeling by my bedside that hot summer night and praying that God would show me where I had hidden my bag. I distinctly remember telling God, "I don't know where I left my bag, but I know that you do, because you know all things." After that, I cried myself to sleep. It was then that God revealed to me, through a dream, exactly where my little bag containing the newly purchased items was. Upon awakening, with joyful screams and hollers, I climbed to the exact ceiling beam I had dreamed about. The family must have thought I had gone insane as I yelled out, "I knew it! I knew it!" I trusted that God knew exactly where I had hidden my bag and how much it meant to me. What an impact God made on my life that day!

The next day as we were crossing the Rio Grande River and driving into Mexico, I was ready for surgery. Everything went well—just a little scar and a short, two-day stay in the hospital. Today, I still have the scar, but more important, an everlasting memory lined my heart with the wonderful experience I had with Almighty God.

I have to acknowledge that something different—special—happened to me as I was growing up. My sister Carmen, age eleven, didn't have time to notice what I was experiencing. Being the eldest, she had to help Mom with her other eight siblings ranging from age nine to two. After me, all were born just one year apart. Hilda hung around with Ayola—simple "Ay" as we call her now. Both were too busy playing and annoying my three brothers, who were younger than them and preferred to keep to themselves. Then there were Anita and Melva—still babies and certainly too young to know what was going on with the rest of the family. Mom and Dad did see God's grace in my life, but not knowing enough to identify it as such, simply claimed that I was the smartest and the most outspoken of the four eldest. Carmen was very timid and shy, and the other two were younger than me, so by default, I became the family's spokesperson and errand runner. Maybe it was my adventurous spirit or my extroverted character that led to my many special experiences. What is undoubted is that God's grace in my life gave way to many unforgettable manifestations.

On my tenth birthday, our family doctor and his wife came to our house out in the country to drop off a birthday cake for me. I must have been the one taken to their office most often, because somehow they knew it was my birthday and surprised us with such a special treat. None of us had ever had a birthday cake, and birthdays were just not celebrated. My dad, a hardworking, illiterate farmer who could barely write his name, was too busy working the farm to bother with birthdays. Mom could read and write both English and Spanish but was so busy raising nine kids that birthdays were the last thing on her mind. Besides, we couldn't afford cakes, much less parties, and no one really cared until that day: April 26, 1954.

Carmen started baking cakes for us from that day on, and Mom would sew new dresses for us girls or new shirts for the boys on our birthdays. My parents' birthdays, however, were never mentioned. That nice gesture from our family physician had made a difference in my family. I still ask myself, Why me? Why not show up on Carmen's, Hilda's, or anyone else's birthday? Why me? Whatever the answer, I choose to believe that it was God's special way of dealing with a ten-year-old that He was preparing for great challenges ahead.

Growing Up to Greater Experiences

Christmas of 1956 was an exceptionally good one for me. There I was, a twelve-year-old in the sixth grade, coming home with three gifts instead of just one like everyone else. I didn't pay much attention to the present I had received in class. I was more interested in showing off a delicate miniature china set and a doll that two friends, who were high school seniors, had given me. To my surprise, my dad ordered me to put them away and not play with them until after the holidays were over when we would go back to school and Carmen could verify that the gifts had indeed been given to me. My parents didn't believe in this "luck" business. I cried in disbelief that my parents didn't trust me. Did they not see Jesus in my life? I was a Christian, and Christians didn't lie or steal!

As if receiving three gifts at school hadn't been enough trouble for me, on Sunday all of us were given Christmas gifts at church too. Again, all were given one gift, and for a reason I'll never know, I was given two very special gifts. I still remember a pair of white gloves and a little blue box purse with a small fruit arrangement that decorated the lid. Of course, this time, my parents didn't say a word because all nine of us had gone to Sunday school together—and those *were* my gifts.

As we got off the bus for the first day after the Christmas holidays, my two senior friends were waiting for me and asked me, in front of Carmen, how I had liked the "tea set and the doll." With that, Carmen breathed a sigh of relief because she wouldn't have to investigate. When we got home that afternoon, Carmen, embarrassed by the mission but happy to report the truth, clarified to my parents that the gifts had indeed been given to me. Now I could play with the miniature tea set and doll. I remember being so angry at my parents for doubting me that I went out back to the outhouse and disposed of the little doll. I didn't even play with it once. How sad! As for my little tea set, I preserve it in my china cabinet as one of my treasured possession of nearly sixty years.

Me at age twelve.

One of my greatest earthly treasures, this miniature teacup set was a special Christmas gift when I was only twelve years old. Nearly sixty years later, it remains in mint condition.

What does a birthday cake or some Christmas gifts have to do with angels? First, I believe God sometimes uses average, normal, everyday folk to send a message telling us we're special. I choose to call that kind of messenger an angel, whether he or she realizes it or not. Second, could those two girls have been real angels? Why would two seniors want to socialize or hang around with a sixth grader? And where were they the rest of the year? Why can't I recognize them in the school yearbook pictures? I don't understand, but I do thank God for that special Christmas, because it would mark the first of many to remember.

A Teenager in Love

At age sixteen, I was a high school sophomore in love. Even though my plans were to elope with my boyfriend on my next birthday, everything came to a halt when Mom pulled me out of school due to severe problems with my eyesight. A medical leave of absence was granted for only the month of December; therefore, I would have to be back at school after the Christmas holidays. In the meantime, our Pentecostal Christian friends (the Gracia family) from Brownsville, Texas, offered me a job at the hospital where two of them, Angelica and Gloria, worked—just across the street from their house. They even offered for me to stay and live with them while working. My parents agreed. I enjoyed my job in the pediatrics department.

On Christmas day, my boyfriend surprised me with a very special gift: a set of rings and a watch—a Baylor watch. *Is this guy crazy?* I thought. *Does he actually think I will go home displaying the engagement and wedding rings?* I shared my problem with Angelica, Gloria, and Elizabeth (the youngest of the three Gracia girls). Surely they would have a solution to my dilemma. At first they were tickled because they knew my boyfriend, but later they became concerned knowing how strict my parents were. After weighing all the options, the only solution that would really work required for me to lie to my parents about the Christmas presents.

My friends insisted there was nothing wrong with lying for a justifiable reason, and not having another route to take, I decided to lie to my mom and my family. I honestly didn't care if I lied to my dad because at that age, I had become resentful toward him for the family problems we were facing. The plan the girls and I concocted was sure to work. I gave my boyfriend the rings to keep until we would elope in a few months. As for the Baylor watch, I made up a story about having won it in a raffle at the hospital where I was working. Mom and the family bought the story. What a lucky girl I was—or so they thought. As with all fairy tales, the plot thickened. The lucky girl became a miserable one soon thereafter.

Three months later, I broke up with my first love—my very first boyfriend—and angrily gave him back the watch. I emphatically told him my decision was final. Breaking up wasn't as bad as having to lie again. How would I explain the loss of the watch? I would have to say I had lost my watch at school. I was crying when I got home due to the breakup, but everyone thought it was because I had lost my watch! Mom was so sorry about my misfortune that she was willing to send word to the school principal and offer a five-dollar or ten-dollar reward if it was found. That was a lot of money for a low-income family in 1961. Lying to her really hurt me. How many more lies would it take, and how long would this go on? I was supposed to be a Christian and wasn't supposed to lie—period!

That night, all I could think of was suicide. That, I thought, would end my misery. The day came when I literally picked up my dad's rifle and thought I'd end it all. With the rifle in hand, I couldn't do it. Not because I couldn't pull the trigger, but because I couldn't leave Mom behind suffering the loss of a daughter in addition to all her personal problems with Dad. Who was going to defend her or stand by her if things got worse between them? Carmen, though the eldest, was terrified when she'd hear them quarreling and pretended she was asleep to avoid mingling in the heated debates, and the rest of the family was younger and couldn't interject even if they had wanted to. My life changed in that very moment. I put down the rifle and dropped to my knees. Instead of committing suicide, I recommitted my life to Jesus, my Lord and Savior.

I thanked God for Mom's prayers on my behalf. She had requested prayer from my pastor and from other close friends. She knew something was happening in my life but would have never suspected I was having suicidal thoughts. Prayer spared my life, and I can truly say today that there would not be a story to tell had the angel of God not been there to stop me from harming myself.

The bad experiences were quickly overshadowed by the Easter events of 1961 and my seventeenth birthday. What an unforgettable Easter. I had not been allowed to get baptized at age nine, but now I knew exactly what I wanted with my life. I wanted to be a Christian and live for the God that had forgiven my lies and cleansed me of all my sins. I asked Mom to forgive me, and in one church service, I made a public confession of how the Devil had set the trap with the purpose of destroying me—and of how God had spared my life.

That Easter was a true celebration for our family, because all four of us older girls were baptized the same day. (We had been baptized in the Catholic church as babies, but now we were getting baptized as adults, meaning we were publicly confessing a personal decision to receive Jesus as our Lord and Savior and take a stand to live for Him for the rest of our lives.) Years later, Mom and the boys were baptized also, followed by Anita and Melva. Dad was never baptized, although he did have the blessed opportunity of accepting Christ into his heart seven years later, one week before he died. I feel peace and assurance of his welcome into his heavenly home and look forward to seeing him when we all meet again someday. As for my seventeenth birthday, I had absolutely no regrets about having ended my relationship with my boyfriend a month and twenty-one days before the scheduled date of our eloping. God had restored my life and had helped me defeat the Enemy. Now that I had victory, my only focus was to graduate from high school and go on to college.

Folktales and Angels

After graduation in May 1963, I held a temporary job at a shrimp-packing company in Port Isabel, Texas, a small town adjacent to the famous and only real amusement of the Rio Grande Valley: the beach of South Padre Island. Its beaches are indeed a tourist attraction. Attraction or not, I hated my job at the shrimp-packing factory where my sisters Carmen and Hilda worked. I made matters worse by telling myself that I had not received a high school diploma to work on a shrimp line. Carmen was also a high school graduate, but she vouched she would never hold another book in her hands, much less consider going to college. Hilda had dropped out of high school and was glad she had a job instead of staying at home. They both seem to enjoy their work and had friends there, but I disliked it so much that, quite frankly, I wasn't doing well or meeting the manager's minimum expectations—on purpose. After putting up with me for two weeks, moving me from line to line to see where I could cut it, she had to let me go. I rejoiced at the action taken. Firing me was an answered prayer and a huge blessing. As for the boss that fired me, *she* was my angel for the day.

CHAPTER 3

No College on the Horizon

After graduating from high school, one is expected to work or go to college. For me, though, the prospect of going to Baylor University in Waco became more and more remote as the days went by. My eyesight had worsened, and I was literally, clinically, going blind. My parents would not let me go away to study, although a part of me thought it was for the better because the problems between them had escalated and I needed to stay home and help Mom. My dream of college was put on hold. Oh, how I prayed.

The Baylor watch my boyfriend had given me had inspired my choice for a university. I wasn't totally informed about the school itself; I just related it to a gift I'd received two years prior. I never considered applying to any other university. I was accepted, and even sent in my deposit to hold my spot, but it soon became obvious that college was nowhere near in my future.

Would I ever become the stenographer I wanted to be? Not if I didn't go to college, and not until my family would stop feeling sorry for me. I was becoming ever so irritable and useless with everybody pitying me. My eyesight was so bad that I couldn't even do house chores or read—and I loved reading. I would even hide from my parents to do just that, but the pain in my eyes, from straining to see the small letters, was what I had to negotiate with. Sometimes, I could read a few minutes and no more. Other times, I could go on for hours, but I knew I would pay for it later with extended periods of throbbing pain behind my eyes. I thank God that the day came when I was prayed for at church and God healed me. I didn't ask God for perfect vision. I just wanted to be able to see better and read for hours—pain free. He healed me and I was finally free from the pain that strained my eyeballs.

Sun Rays at Last

The summer of 1964 was a breakthrough time for me. God started to pour out blessings and miracles upon Mom through unexpected opportunities for work and other demonstrations of His care for her. All of us, including Mom, had forgiven Dad and felt peace with him for his mistakes that ended their relationship in a divorce. He continued living alone, living his life, while Mom had major decisions to make. The Lord just took control of our household, making things finally fall into place. I'm convinced that He sent angels to lead us from a dark place in the family's history to one of brightness.

Someone from church, out of pity I'm sure, seeing a woman in her mid-forties alone with nine children (most in their teens), convinced Mom to make a trip up north as migrant workers along with his family. Brother Hernandez would contract and transport families to Michigan to work in the fields. Of course we were used to working in the fields—hoeing or picking cotton—but not thinning beets, picking cherries, or harvesting tomatoes. The idea sounded like fun. A typical migrant family's work was to last all summer, moving from job site to job site, in fields from Michigan to Ohio—one week working one fruit or vegetable and the next a different one. After some coaxing and with the promising outlook of earning a lot of money, and the promise that Brother Hernandez would loan us a car, Mom agreed for us to go only for the first leg of the trip—with no obligation to follow the crew to all the job sites the whole summer. My younger siblings had to be back in time for school. School was one thing Mom would not compromise on. So after signing a contract, all nine of us and Mom would soon be Michigan bound.

Brother Hernandez, the foreman and contractor for one of the sugar-beets companies in Sebewaing, Michigan, had been extra nice when he offered his car for us to drive while he drove his big truck where he carried other families. My brothers would take turns riding in the truck, as the car wasn't big enough for a family of ten. We were off on a new adventure.

We hated to leave Dad behind. Leaving him was especially hard for Mom who was battling her own emotions and seeing my brothers and two younger sisters cry and worry about him staying alone. We four older girls were strong for Mom. Sister Maria Hernandez, Brother Hernandez's wife, together with all the crew, would pray for us and offered comforting words as we drove away and got on the road for our first destination. The trip from the valley would last two and a half days.

After arriving in Michigan, we started working, and things started to get better. The kids would occasionally mention Dad and cry and be saddened, but we all prayed ourselves through those hard emotional times. The Lord was good. It seemed like God had sent very special people to assist Mom in everything we had to do. He gave us grace with the beets company's contractors. Instead of placing us in a cottage in the "camp" where all the other families lived, we were given a house to ourselves. Instead of working in the fields with all the other migrant families, we were given our own fields. Brother Hernandez even turned over to Mom and Carmen the sole responsibility of seeking out the fields we would work on next and deal directly with the field owners. Mom was our only foreman—forewoman, that is. Of course God knew exactly what He was doing. He was paving the way for the days and years ahead.

Hoeing and thinning beet fields was different work from what we were used to back home. Here, we had a contract and were working and being paid by the acre and not on a daily or hourly basis. Only Mom and Carmen knew what terms were in the contract that had been signed before we left Texas. All I knew was that at the end of the season, we were supposed to get a bonus check of some kind. The truth of the matter is that we didn't do as well as we had hoped for, resulting in us not earning the money we had expected. Because we didn't meet the acreage quota, we didn't get the bonus check either.

Mom was very disappointed but had to be brave for our sake. We didn't make enough money to cover our trip expenses which had been advanced to us by the beets company. To top it off, all Mom had in the bank back home was fifty dollars. Our only choice was to continue with the crew to their next migratory stop, moving on to Ludington, Michigan, for cherry picking. Having learned to rely on God, we cried and prayed, prayed and cried. Maybe things would be better in Ludington. Holding back our tears, we traveled with the group, experiencing firsthand a typical migrant family's yearly trip. Most of the families in the crew had done this for years. They would go from job to job and from state to state doing this kind of labor. Not us. We didn't even know if we would like picking cherries or harvesting tomatoes.

Once in Ludington, things started going wrong with the Hernandez family. All of a sudden, their attitude changed toward Mom. Was it because we were doing better than everyone else in the crew in the cherry-picking business? It had turned out to be fun work. We were actually enjoying it! A spirit of jealousy, however, separated the Hernandez from Mom. Adding to Mom's burden, a relative of theirs warned her of Brother Hernandez's intentions of taking back the car he had loaned us, leaving us stranded when they would move on to Ohio for the tomato harvest. Another family advised Mom to purchase a vehicle. Brother Ayala had just purchased a pickup truck at a dealership in downtown Ludington where he had traded in his old one in the process. Maybe Mom could buy his old truck, for as little as what he had gotten for it in the trade-in. The bad news crushed our spirit. We all prayed and humbled ourselves before the Lord. We pleaded for

His intervention. Surely, He would have the answer to our problem by morning.

As brave as a woman has to be in a time of crisis, Mom got up the following morning ready to face the challenges of the day. She was determined to take the bull by the horns and follow the directions of the Holy Spirit. With a strong heart and a bold face, she asked that Carmen and me go with her to the business district in Ludington. She sent the rest of the family to the cherry trees that were assigned to us for the day. Brother and Sister Ayala would supervise the family while we were gone.

Brother Ayala had given us directions to the dealership where he had traded in his truck. We had no problem getting to the location of that beautiful city, even though it was the first time we had gone into downtown. No sooner were we at the dealership than Carmen and I, instead of going to the used cars lot, insisted on going to see a gorgeous, aqua-blue pickup truck in the showroom. Mom tried to stop us, telling us we were crazy and that we had come only to inquire about Ayala's old truck. We were so awestruck at the sight of the new pickup truck that we weren't listening to her. We kept walking toward the window where we were greeted by a very nice gentleman.

Mom explained the reason for our visit that we were there to inquire about a used truck brought to his dealership days before. Carmen and I must have distracted the salesman with our insistence on Mom to at least look into buying the new truck. He politely dismissed Mom's objections to ignore us. He ushered us to his office and picked up the phone. Before we could even whisper a prayer or say amen, he was talking to someone at the Muskegon, Michigan, dealership office. All I remember him saying over the phone is "I have a young lady with two beautiful daughters sitting in my office interested in the pickup in the showroom." I don't know what else they discussed. All I know is that he started pulling up papers and asking Mom to sign in the spaces he indicated. Mom was speechless. She told him she didn't have but fifty dollars in a bank account back home in Texas and that we hadn't earned much in Sebewaing. The salesman turned a deaf ear to all she was saying and proceeded with the paperwork. "Just sign here, ma'am," he said.

Why Mom signed those papers, I'll never know. I don't think she even knew how to start to mount a protest to such an unthinkable transaction. I remember the mixed emotions visible on Mom's face when the salesman, with a big grin on his face, handed Mom the keys to not just any brand-new 1964 Chevrolet C-10 pickup truck but the very one Carmen and I had just seen in the showroom! The nice gentleman, our angel, saw us off, and we headed back to camp with a brand-new vehicle. Were we shocked? Of course we were shocked, but our hearts were also rejoicing, praising God for such a miracle. No money down and whatever payment arrangements were made, only God and Mom knew. Mom could worry about that later.

When we got to camp, the whole world, or so it seemed, came out to greet us. Mom asked everyone to hold hands and to surround the truck while she issued a beautiful prayer thanking God for the miracle before our very eyes. As for the borrowed car, we surrendered it before Brother Hernandez could even ask for it.

Then it was time to hit the trees—return to work, I mean—and continue with the cherry picking. I dare say we picked more bushels the next day than ever before. And rightly so, because we were experiencing happiness once again! The dark clouds of anguish, disappointments, and humiliations seemed to have lifted away in a moment. God's beautiful rays of hope shone like never before in our lives.

When the owner of the cherry orchard learned about our miracle, he and his wife took it upon themselves to park our truck in their garage, lest someone would purposely scratch it again, as had happened that very first night. They couldn't believe someone could do such a thing! The couple kept the truck in their garage and, because we were so busy working to be paying attention to our truck, were able to give us a huge surprise the day before we left their field. They had purchased a camper for our truck—installed and road ready!

Had God instructed them to do it? Or did they care that we were leaving the next day and that most of our family would be riding in the back, on the bed of the truck? The reason for their generous gesture was a wonderful mystery to Mom, to all nine of us, and to the other families at the camp. The Hernandez were back in talking terms and had reconciled with Mom and us. They too confessed they had never seen this sort of generosity expressed at their camp before, nor had any boss or owner done anything special for any family for as long as they could recall. What a miracle!

Despite the wonderful memories, we never went back to cherry picking. We didn't like tomato picking in Ohio either. We managed to leave the tomato camp before Brother Hernandez and his crew did. We stayed in Ohio for about a week or two then headed for our home in Texas. Carmen was an excellent driver, and in the brand-new 1964 C-10 pickup truck, she certainly was a much happier and grateful one.

God's New Plans Revealed

We had enjoyed the summer of 1964 despite the unpleasant moments we had experienced. We returned home in time for school for my younger brothers and sisters. Dad was happy that we were back, and we were overjoyed to see him too. The trip up north had been the inspiration we all needed to finally move away from a country life to seek better jobs and opportunities in the city. Because "the city" for us was Brownsville, only twenty miles from Los Fresnos, we would still be able to see Dad. Moving there offered another benefit: we would be much closer to church and to our Christian friends.

It wasn't long before Mom heard that a house was for sale on Avalon Drive in Brownsville. I believe Mr. Hermosa, the seller, was another angel waiting to carry out orders from our heavenly Father. The sale was a breeze. Mom had the money for the down payment and we were confident we could handle the payments. We felt good about the deal and trusted that we would earn enough money to pay the note in full come the summer after we went up north again. As I consider the blessings we received that year, I praise God that in a one-year period, the Lord gave us a new pickup truck and a new house in Brownsville. What a mighty God we serve!

Our house in Brownsville, Texas, where Mom lived
until she went home to be with Jesus.

The following summer, with the benefit of one summer experience, we considered ourselves official migrant workers. Our family returned to Sebewaing, Michigan, where we found comfort in seeing the familiar faces of our Mennonite friends and of those in the Assembly of God church we had attended while there the year before. That summer, the Mennonites loaned us their small mission church building named Fairhaven, so that we could have our Spanish church services. Migrant workers filled the little church. Some of our Mennonite friends even stayed after their own Sunday school service to join us. Though none knew a word of Spanish, they loved our songs. They enjoyed watching my brothers play the guitars and were impressed with our form of worship, which included clapping of hands and the playing of tambourines as we sang along.

At the time, I didn't yet know how to preach and would actually just read a passage of Scripture and explain it. God's spirit would, however, make itself present in those gatherings and we enjoyed having good old-fashioned Pentecostal services. They were just what we, the "Holy Rollers," as we were called back then, needed, because we would leave the little country church every Sunday ready to meet the challenges of the week with renewed faith and overwhelming joy.

Soon thereafter, God started placing on my heart a call to prepare for the ministry. I fought with God's calling, refusing to acknowledge it. I still looked forward to going to college and becoming a stenographer someday, not a preacher. The fact that I was preaching at Fairhaven on Sundays was only because I had been put on the spot, not because I wanted to be a preacher. I had other plans, plans to move to Waco, because I had not forgotten Baylor!

God changed my plans altogether, and as soon as we got back home that year, in the fall of 1965, I enrolled in a two-year program at Bethel Bible Institute in Harlingen, Texas, to prepare for the ministry. I kept going up north with my family to work in the fields every summer, even after graduating from Bible school in May 1967.

During the summer of 1967, while working in Michigan, I felt like I needed to do more for the Lord and planned my first missionary trip. The plan was to come home to give my very first vacation Bible school ("VBS") in my home church, then travel to Ciudad Juarez, Mexico, to hold one there too. A friend I had not seen for two years had invited me to go and give a VBS in her church. My only obstacle was this: would Mom let me go? Although I was an adult, I was still bound by my cultural restraints requiring parental permission for big decisions. I could almost hear the nays. "What about the rest of the family who has to stay behind and continue working in the fields?" It was not an easy decision for Mom, but our Mennonite friends, especially the Glen Maust and Paul Gingerich families, who were strong believers in missions, not only convinced Mom to let me go but also contributed VBS supplies and sponsored my very first missionary trip. Everyone in my family seemed to accept the idea, and soon after, I took a bus from Michigan to Texas. Sure, it was a long three-day trip, but I was the happiest "missionary" on board.

CHAPTER 4

A Missionary at Last

The vacation Bible school session at my church was a tremendous success. We had over one hundred children. I even called the local newspaper to come take pictures and write an article about our very first VBS at Templo Sinai of Brownsville. Next was my trip to Mexico. I had never traveled into Mexico, besides the occasional trip to the doctor, but that was just across the river to the border town of Matamoros and back. I also had not heard from my friend, Margarita Guerrero, in two years. All she had ever given me was a phone number, and only God knew if by that date it was a working number or not. Determined to find out for myself whether all this pounding in my heart was from God or coming from my own emotions, I prayed for a miracle. I needed confirmation regarding my call to the ministry. I needed the Lord's angels to take me to Mexico if God really wanted me there.

I was living with our oldest and dearest Christian friends, Baltazar and Angelica García, because my family was still in Michigan and I didn't want to stay at home alone. One day, after Sunday school, I was desperate to talk to God. The Garcías had errands to run but dropped me off at their home at my request. I quickly locked myself in the bedroom, fell to my knees, and started praying and weeping, determined not to let up until I had a definite answer from God. After a while, I felt led to call the only phone number I had for Margarita. I placed the call to Ciudad Juarez, Mexico.

Lo and behold, the phone was ringing! That meant at least that it was a working number! Just as quickly as it was heightened, my spirit sank when there was no answer. I made a final attempt and let it ring about twenty times, or so it seemed. "One more time," I'd tell myself with deep disappointment. Just as I was getting ready to hang up, someone answered. I couldn't believe it! I could hardly contain my heart in my chest. I finally got a hold of myself and was able to speak to the gentleman who answered.

The person at the other end happened to be a Methodist minister answering the phone inside the church office. He later told us that while preparing for the night's sermon in his study at home, which was adjacent to the church building, he'd felt the Lord urging him to go to the church office. He couldn't explain why God wanted him to go, but he went anyway. After I explained the purpose for my call, he told me he was shocked at the way the Lord had "moved" and practically lifted him up from his chair and taken him to the building next door. He told of how, as he approached the door, he could hear the phone ringing in his office and rushed to answer it before the ringing stopped. He explained that it had to have been the Lord's doing, because he normally didn't allow anyone to interrupt him while preparing a sermon.

After giving the minister my phone number where Margarita could reach me, he promised to personally go look for her after church that evening and relay the message. (He knew the family but hadn't seen them or gone out to their place for some time.) He said he'd even offer to take Margarita from Ciudad Juarez across the border to El Paso, Texas, to pick me up whenever I would decide to visit. By now he was curious and wanted to meet the young lady with whom God was so strongly dealing.

Margarita called me the following day and the plans were squared away. She had spoken to her pastor, the Reverend Luciano Avitia, about

A Missionary at Last

me and would be waiting for me to arrive to give the first vacation Bible school in the history of their church.

I set off for El Paso the following week. The middle-aged Methodist minister, together with Margarita and her brother Miguel, greeted me at the bus station, took us back to Juarez, and I never saw or heard from the minister again. No one mentioned him again after that day either. *Weird*, I thought, but deep inside, I knew he had been the angel God had used to confirm my true calling to the ministry.

That summer, together with my missionary friends Margarita Guerrero or Mage and Maria Elena Avitia or Nena, I held a VBS at three different locations. Each is burned in my memory for distinct reasons. At the first of the schools, which was at Brother Avitia's church, a little girl about nine or ten years old collapsed during one of our classes. Pastor Avitia, a man who was constantly fasting and praying, came to assist. He prayed and declared healing for the child. By the end of the week, we had news from the child's grandmother that not only had the child been previously diagnosed with leukemia but also that the Lord had healed her granddaughter; she had been given a clean bill of health after we prayed for her. What a miracle!

At the second location, a twelve-year-old boy with an inexplicable look of a child criminal (in my opinion) caught my attention. When Mage overheard my remark about his looks, she explained that he, in fact, had recently killed his younger brother. His grandmother who was very old had told the police it had all been an accident, even though it had actually happened in a moment of rage. I felt God was reaching out to this child, so I went over to the fence where he would stand day after day watching the VBS children doing all kinds of arts and crafts. After inviting him to join us to help with the crafts, he accepted and even promised to go help at our next VBS. It was there, at Sister Ruiz's church, that God saved this innocent killer. He wept and wept during the sermon. Then, falling to his knees with his face to the floor, he begged for forgiveness and cried till he could cry no more. When asked if he wanted to commit his life to Jesus, his answer was yes. The change was obvious. His face was radiant and didn't have that mean, criminal look anymore. That was the turning point for this young man's life. Years later, I learned that he had been baptized and had gone with Brother Avitia to the mountains in Chihuahua to aid in a mission where he eventually stayed to pastor.

From left to right: Margarita Guerrero, me, and Maria Elena Avitia.

One of my missionary trips to Mexico as we waited to board a bus. Nena Avitia (left) and Mage Guerrero

The third VBS we held was deep in the mountains in Allende, Chihuahua, in a small community called Tres Castillos. We held children's classes in the mornings and revival services in the evenings at all our VBS sites. The greatest miracle there was the reconciliation of our hostess with her twenty-year-old sister. They had lived under the same roof without speaking to each other for months after a heated discussion between them. God saved the younger sister, and peace returned to their home.

Upon witnessing the reconciliation, the hugs, the peace, and the move of God in that little room where we were holding our services, the hostess's brother also came forward and hugged them both. He too surrendered his life to Jesus, and then he rushed to his house only to return with his wife. His wife had been a Christian and a faithful church attendee until she had married him. She had not set foot in a church for seventeen years, because her husband forbade it. With tears in his eyes, he asked her to kneel, and there, kneeling before us as if we were the miracle workers, he begged her forgiveness and promised he would never deprive her from serving God again. We deflected his attention to the Lord who was performing all these breakthroughs in that home before our eyes. With all the wonderful things happening that night, the service was prolonged to almost midnight. We didn't care about the time, because after all, God was doing great things—and that was all that mattered.

We were scheduled to catch the bus to Monterrey, Mexico, the following morning but instead had to reschedule because the people wouldn't let us go. We were insisted upon to wake up early and hold another revival service where people that had initially resisted us, claiming that we were invading a Catholic community, were now surrendering their lives to Jesus. With all the pleasant commotion, the town priest came to see what was going on. After a few words with him, he only had words of praise for our "good work" there.

Mage and I took the bus to Monterrey, while Nena and José, her cousin, rode back to Ciudad Juarez. Mage and I held a VBS in two other villages, one in the Monterrey area and the other in San Luis Potosí, Mexico, where we had a record 126 children in attendance.

The reason that number stuck so vividly in my mind was because on the last day of classes we were forced to dismiss early. It had rained so heavily that we were advised to get out quickly due to the river's rising waters. If we were there after the river's water level rose beyond a certain point, we would be stranded until the water receded days later. As a result, we didn't have time to have the afternoon ceremony with the parents to give out certificates, gifts, and other materials as we always did at the end of each VBS week. We did, however, manage to call the children back early. One by one, and in groups, they came drenched from head to toe. I was so moved in my spirit by that sight that I purposely stepped out into the rain and got drenched myself. Mage did likewise. We had to do it for the kids' sake. That was the most beautiful VBS closing service I have ever had in my life. We gave out the materials and dismissed the children as quickly as possible. The rain stopped for a little while, giving us just enough time for us to leave that community. We left El Charco del Agua, San Luis Potosí, Mexico, with an experience we would treasure for the rest of our lives.

After this missionary trip, I lost contact with Mage and Nena for four decades. And while our lives had taken different paths, each with our own challenges and assignments from God, our reunion forty years later was a testament to how the Lord's calling in our lives to minister was an enduring one. All three of us are still active in ministry, praise God.

A Missionary at Last

From left to right: Maria Elena Avitia, me, and Margarita Guerrero Reunited in 2008, forty years after losing contact.

My missionary trips to the state of Chihuahua continued through 1970. Then the Griffins, an elderly missionary couple, invited me to go give vacation Bible schools in the Saltillo, Mexico, area. There I met Sylvia Juarez, a fourteen-year-old girl I invited to go along with me to help with a children's class. Her parents, who had accompanied the Griffins several times before and knew the area well, allowed her to go along. The VBS classes were a tremendous success, and I returned home praising God for a new missionary partner. Sylvia and I became very close friends and continued going to the mission fields, even after losing contact with the Griffins.

Today, both Sylvia and I are still in the ministry. Our husbands and families have been our strongest supporters. The greatest blessing of our having met is that our children are now good friends. May God continue to bless Sylvia Juarez de Jasso, her husband, Santos Jasso, and their children.

A Mighty Rushing Wind

I never went back to Mexico after my last VBS with Sylvia. Instead I was directed by God to minister in Toledo, Ohio, where my sister Carmen was living at the time. In the summer of 1971, I was invited by her pastor to give the first vacation Bible school at their church. I was also asked to give a workshop to train their Sunday school staff for future Bible summer classes. After a few weeks there, I thought, *Mission accomplished*. It turned out that God was using this training period to cultivate something in my own life as much as in the lives of those Sunday schoolteachers at the seminar.

For me, preaching at revival services every Passion Week was a must. (Passion Week is the week preceding Easter, which, for Pentecostals, is often marked by revival services several days in a row and culminates on Easter Sunday.) Every year since I had graduated from Bible school, I had always had a place to preach during this very important week. In the spring of 1972, however, I found myself crying out to the Lord on the Saturday before Passion Week began because I didn't have a single invitation to preach somewhere during Passion Week. Not having a revival service at which to preach was like a death sentence to my ministry. "Has God rejected me?" I asked. "What has happened to God's grace in my life? And where are the *angels*, the *visions*, and *the revelations* I used to enjoy? Have they become things of the past? What about my relationship with my Lord? Have I grown cold spiritually and not sought Him like before?" I wondered. With so many questions and not enough answers, I turned to God, asking Him to speak to me and show me what to do that Passion Week.

That Saturday night was an exceptionally memorable night. I had been begging God to "open a door" for me somewhere, anywhere, just so that I'd preach on Good Friday and on Easter Sunday. I had been praying, sobbing, and waiting since nine o'clock that night when something absolutely extraordinary happened at around two o'clock Sunday morning.

I had just stopped praying and lain down (I don't know if I fell asleep instantly or had just dosed off) when, suddenly, a mighty rushing wind literally opened a door in my room, which led to the outside of the house. It was a side-entry door which we seldom used. My bedroom was the only one with such a door leading to the outside of the house. A northern wind maybe could justify such a powerful gust, but my room was on the south side of the house and the door was shut tight. Because it was seldom used, no one ever tinkered with the locks keeping it securely closed. It had the knob lock plus three more latches. Mom made sure every door was tightly secured, because by this time, we were only women living alone in this big house. I didn't become frightened or think that someone was trying to break in when the door burst open. I got up, tiptoed to Mom's room, and heard that she was sound asleep (which was unusual for her, because she would normally awaken with the slightest noise).

A sense of peace overtook me. I quietly closed the door, got back on my knees, and started thanking and praising God for the miracle He had just performed. He had quite literally just *opened a door*. No, it wasn't a dream. It wasn't a revelation or an angel which had visited me that night. Instead, God chose to wake me up with a force that was so powerful it opened a secure door yet so gentle that it did not disturb my mother. God Himself had been with me that night. I knew without a shadow of a doubt that the opening of my bedroom door meant God had opened a door for me to go preach the following weekend. I didn't know where, but the worst part of the wait was over. He would take care of the details. With great joy and confidence, I finally called it a night.

I slept sound until six o'clock that morning when the phone rang. Lo and behold, it was my sister Carmen calling me. She immediately broke the news, stating that several pastors had been praying all night and that precisely at two o'clock in the morning the Lord had instructed them to invite me to go minister at their Good Friday Church Rally (where several churches would get together for the event) and to stay for the Easter Sunday sunrise service. She added that the local church would pay for all my expenses to and from Toledo, Ohio.

Friday night was a Holy Ghost and power service. When I was giving testimony of what had happened at home at exactly 2:00 a.m. a week prior, the church pastor rushed to the platform. He asked for the microphone and testified that it was at that precise time that God had also visited them at the altar, where they had been instructed by the Almighty to invite me for the weekend revival. Upon hearing the coinciding testimonies, a mighty spirit force (like the rushing wind on the day of Pentecost, according to the Bible in Acts 2) swept across the auditorium and laid thick upon us all. I had just started preaching and had inserted my testimony when the pastor had come up. After that, the whole congregation gave the Holy Spirit the freedom He deserves. They began to jump and speak in tongues, and some even rolled on the floor—all under the power of the Holy Spirit.

Needless to say, I didn't conclude my sermon, and after a long while of just rejoicing in the Lord, the pastor made a few announcements and dismissed for the night. I preached at the sunrise service on Easter Sunday then immediately flew back home to make it in time for the night service at my home church. How I longed to share God's blessings and unforgettable memories with Mom, my family, and my church.

College Bound

After seven years as a teacher assistant, I decided to go back to school and begin working toward a teaching degree. Ten years had elapsed since my high school graduation before I finally had the opportunity to go to college for two semesters in 1972–1973. Then I received an invitation to teach at a Bible Institute in McAllen, Texas. That meant I had to quit my job with the Brownsville School District and put a hold on my college dream. After seeking advice from Mom and my pastor, the Reverend Tomas Amaya, I accepted the appointments of professor and dean of girls at Berea Bible Institute, where I worked for three years between 1973 and 1976.

A Missionary at Last

While at Berea, the Glen Maust family who lived in Michigan told me about their plans to go to Bogotá, Colombia, in South America. We had met the Mausts and the Paul Gingerich families on our very first trip to Michigan back in the 1960s and they had become very close friends. The Mausts were flying down to Bogotá to visit their son who was doing missionary work with Wycliffe Bible Translators. They invited me to go along to see a different side of missionary work. The trip would be in February, and I was sure the Bible school director would give me a two-week convenience leave. After all, it was for a missionary trip. Mom, on the other hand, was terribly concerned, but after some coaxing, she agreed to let me go with the family that we all loved so dearly. Going with the Maust family to Bogotá was another of God's plans, one that paved the way for a more personal missionary trip later.

Before long, I was packing up to fly to South America to meet with Brother Glen and Sister Erma Maust. After I arrived, I became very interested in the work these missionaries were doing in the area of linguistics and Bible translation into native tribal dialects. I spent most of my time with the local missionary teams and their native translators while the Maust family visited with their son. The two weeks went by fast. I promised I'd pray about returning someday. We flew back home to tell about the beautiful work Wycliffe Bible Translators were doing.

For two years, I had shoved off the idea about returning to Colombia. I honestly refused to go, even though the Lord had been calling me to return on many occasions. The thought of crossing the Andes would make me freeze, but the need to help the gospel reach the natives in such remote places and the guilt that I would feel refusing God's call to serve would pierce my heart. I cried and cried as I heard God's voice calling me to Loma Linda in Villavicencio, Colombia, where Wycliffe had its central office. Tired of resisting God's call to go, but not completely excited either, I figured I would make it hard for God to get me there. I told God to provide the proceeds, because I didn't dare ask Mom or my church to cover my expenses.

Provide the proceeds? God does have mysterious ways of doing just that. A hailstorm damaged my car. After repairing it with my insurance money, I still had three hundred dollars to spare. Before I could go, I needed to send to the Wycliffe office in California a total of five hundred dollars. Where were the other two hundred? Again God intervened in an unusual way. A week later, I received a check in the mail for the exact amount. The check was from the university, reimbursing me for some credit hours I had paid for but didn't take. With the check in hand, I couldn't hide or refuse to go.

God had fulfilled His end of the bargain, and it was evident that He wanted me to go to Colombia. After explaining the whole scenario to Mom and to my pastor, they both felt this was all God's doing and, despite their concern, did not dare interfere. I had their blessing.

I flew to South America for the second time on May 31, 1977. This time I was going all by myself. Who was supposed to pick me up at the airport when no one knew I was even going? Caught up in the moment, I had failed to think that far ahead. I became nervous while en route to Bogotá when that question finally dawned on me. At age thirty-three, could I still rely on my childhood angels? Would they be around to guide and protect me? I shoved off all the questions and just trusted that the God who had sent me there would again take care of the details.

Little did I know that Brother Bill was the missionary in charge of picking me up, as per the Wycliffe office in California. I learned that only after I stepped off the plane and was ready to go through customs. A very happy and loud voice called my full name. "Who in the world would know my name here if not someone from Wycliffe?" I reasoned. Brother Bill was waiting for me and seven other "summer visitors" who were also going to Loma Linda. Once there, the seven visitors were housed together in a separate building, while I was assigned to an older lady by the name of Sister Greta who lived alone with her beloved cat. I know we should care for all of God's creatures, but oh, how I hated cats. In a few weeks, though, I would learn to love that cat.

I was under the impression that the five hundred dollars I had sent to Wycliffe covered the flight plus room and board. Mom had given me some cash to take along and my church had also given me a small offering, but the good Lord knew that was just enough for my personal expenses. My heart sank when I learned that I had to pay extra for room and board, for personal trips to Villavicencio, and for flight fares on the private planes the missionaries used. Of course, this makes sense now, but then, I was just a wide-eyed, unwary missionary. Although I didn't panic because I knew I could trust the Lord to provide, at that moment, I needed His provision to kick in mighty fast. I prayed and cried myself to sleep that first night. I knew God had not taken me all the way to South America to leave me stranded. Something had to give.

The Lord heard my cry and in a God way proved to me that my stay in Loma Linda was all His doing and not mine. The following day, Sister Greta asked if I could house-sit while she was gone. She was unexpectedly being sent to Panama for two weeks to assist another missionary. She added that if I was willing to care for her beloved cat that she would take care of all my meals at the "comisario" (cafeteria) during the rest of my stay and would even arrange for my flights in and out of Loma Linda! As much as I hated cats, how could I refuse? I probably took better care of that Siamese cat than even Sister Greta ever did. That cat had been my answered prayer.

For two weeks, I worked in an office typing Bible scripts in ten different languages, which the linguists had translated for their respective tribes. Some missionaries were working on the New Testament for the Güahibo tribe. Others needed help setting up manuscripts in the Tucano or Güayabero dialects. I felt good with this humble contribution.

When Sister Greta returned, I was asked to go to the jungles for two weeks. One of the missionaries there had become ill and was being flown back to Bogotá. Wycliffe rules stated that the other lady couldn't stay in the field alone, so I was asked to fill in. My stay among the Tucano Indians was stupendous. I enjoyed every minute of the first week, but once the excitement was over, I was desperate to get out. The heavy rains had caused delays and the plane was unable to fly in to get me back to Loma Linda. I started to worry about Mom and the family. I hadn't called home since I'd left the base, and the only other means of communication was a ham radio, which was inoperable due to the weather. My nerves flared and I started hallucinating, thinking that I'd end up dying in the jungles. What about the other summer visitors? Why weren't any of them asked to come along with me? Besides, I was much farther away from the base in Acaricuara, Vaupés, Colombia, than I had bargained for. Before long, I just wanted out—period.

A Wycliffe plane was finally able to fly into the Tucano jungle airstrip. Sister Claude was flown in and the pilot and I flew back to Loma Linda. Once more, it was only he and I, just as when I had been flown in. The explanation for the delay in retrieving me was that, due to the rainy season, they had been unable to take supplies to the missionaries in Acaricuara and other surrounding areas. They needed every inch in the plane for cargo. So I enjoyed the pilot's conversation going and coming. He too was a summer volunteer, piloting for Wycliffe.

When I got back to Loma Linda, I found out the other seven US summer visitors from the east coast had taken a short trip to a much closer jungle to visit the Corregüaje Tribe. Their plane had engine problems, and totally unprepared to spend the night there, the city girls were forced to do so. I remember hearing how upset they were the following morning when they got back to base. They were complaining about not having their toothbrushes or their makeup with them. I, on the other hand, grateful to be back from roughing it in the jungle, didn't complain. I was glad my plane made it back without any problems and was ready to go back home. I'd been away for two months and Mom must have been dead worried.

Once at base, I immediately called home and gave her the details of my return flight. I was anxious to return home to share all the marvelous things the Lord had done for me in that unforgettable missionary trip.

CHAPTER 5

Angels Explain God's "No"

The year was 1976, and by all indications, I still didn't have time to think about Dora. I didn't stop to think about myself or my future in spite of the fact that some people would joke and mock because I was getting older and everyone around me was getting married, including six of my siblings. I pretended the jokes didn't hurt, but way deep inside, I really wished God would give me the privilege of getting married. Little did I know that I was about to start a love chapter in my life, not as a smitten sixteen-year-old anymore but as a mature young lady in her thirties.

It had been almost two years since our two young missionary friends had been in Brownsville. One was from Mexico, and the other was from the States. Both were handsome and excellent preachers who had, for years, paired up to give revivals in the Brownsville area. While doing so, Mom would house them and provide transportation to the locations where they preached. It was in one of those visits that the gentleman from Mexico mentioned his interest in me but could not betray Mom's trust by asking me to be more than just a friend to him. Uncomfortable with the reaction my mom and family would have if I confessed my feelings for him too, I pretended the feelings were not mutual, but once he left, I really cried out to the Lord. Here was the ideal man for me, I thought, with all the qualities a Christian woman would ever want, and I couldn't have him.

Somehow, Mom could tell of my interest in this young man and would sometimes comment how scared she'd be if any one of us girls still at home would marry a Mexican who would move us away to Mexico. I turned a deaf ear to those comments because I was no longer simply interested in this preacher; I had fallen in love with him.

Mercy! I never wanted this to happen. Besides, he wasn't even aware of my feelings for him, unless he could just tell when he'd stop by to visit. Anyway, I started praying and even crying for this man. I got to the point where I even became angry at God for not answering my prayers. I felt I was ready to get married, and moving across the border was the least of my problems. As long as God would give me this man, I'd be happy. God's answer to my prayers, however, was a clear and plain "No." Naturally, I didn't like God's answer and entered a state of resentment toward God. "Why would He say no?" I asked. My married brothers and sisters had not even bothered to pray yet they'd gotten married. And here I was asking God for His approval and consent, and His answer was flatly "No." That didn't make any sense, and more important, it didn't fit with my intentions of getting on with my life.

I longed to see "my preacher," and when he did stop by the house on his visits to the different churches in Brownsville or in the valley, he'd invite me to preach at his church in Mexico. As a pastor, he was tending to his church in addition to tending to several missions. He insisted that he could use my help. I never once went or accepted his invitation, lest I would insinuate something unfitting for a Christian single. I'd been brought up very modest, and my personal convictions wouldn't allow me to even hint that I was in love with him. I felt that I had to hide my feelings from him for fear they would be transparent. I would be embarrassed if he would find out or see anything in me that would reveal my real feelings. Inside me, however, God knew his offer was tempting, if only for a chance to be near him. I was resigned, therefore, to keep my feelings secret and my fantasies suppressed.

Not surprisingly, nothing was happening in my life as far as a relationship with my preacher man and my attitude with God changed.

Angels Explain God's "No"

In a childish response to God's failure to see things my way, I got mad and wouldn't even pray anymore. I would only think my prayers when I knelt before Him, but I refused to open my mouth. This attitude continued for a while until the Lord intervened in the most unusual way. He sent two angels directly to Brownsville to deliver a heavenly message.

One Sunday night during that very hot summer, two Anglo ladies stepped into our very small church: Templo Sinai on Palm Boulevard and St. Francis Street in Brownsville. They stated that they had seen our church advertised in the local newspaper and that they were visiting us that day to carry out a mission from God. Without more, they sat and worshiped with us until the end of the service. After church, they approached me and asked if I knew of an ice-cream parlor where we could go to sit and talk. There was an ice-cream parlor just behind my house, so we went. None of us at church knew these ladies but they were missionary visitors, so Mom didn't object for me to join them that night. Later they told me that they had singled me out from the youth group that had gone up to sing a special song.

As soon as we got to the parlor, they confronted me politely but very seriously and directly. One of the ladies, the taller one of the two, looked me in the eye and told me, "Our mission has to do with you and a young man in Mexico." How in the world would outsiders know about my life? Besides, I always thought that God was too busy to be mingling with such topics. God had bigger and better things to think about, and these boy-girl relationships were so childish that God would never pay attention to such nonsense, I thought. I was speechless. The other lady broke the silence by saying, "We know he lives in such and such a place and we are going there tomorrow. We will bring you word of his whereabouts. We will meet with you here tomorrow night and inform you of what God has done for you." They said they'd go and come the same day. After all, the place was only three to four hours away and their mission was not to go spend the night but to go and come back immediately. I honestly didn't know what to say or do.

Angels By The Roadside

The ladies weren't asking me for information; they were informing me of their mission. With a God-ordained confidence, they assured me that He would place angels by the roadside to guide them. Still unable to wrap my head around what I was hearing, my most primitive reflex went into hyper mode; I ate that ice-cream cone faster than I had anticipated. We said our good-byes and they said they'd see me the following day. I never did learn their names, nor did they tell me where they were from. When I asked, one replied, "You can call me Sister Jane, and this is Sister Mary. We do not have a home or an address; we travel all over the world." They did mention that they had just come from England, where they'd been on another mission.

When I got home, I didn't say a word to Mom or to my sister Melva. I went straight to my room and started praying. I really prayed this time and didn't feel angry at God anymore. I just felt numb. Surely God would acknowledge my tears and answer my prayers, I thought. Did this mean He would give me the man of my dreams? I must have prayed for hours. I was dumbfounded. Who were these messengers, and why were they going through so much trouble when they didn't even know me?

The following day, they swung by my house only to invite me to the ice-cream parlor again so that we could talk. I rode with them. The two ladies were driving an old, faded maroon car. The window in the driver's side didn't roll up or down, and the air conditioner didn't work. To drive in such a car in the peak of the summer was almost cruel, I thought, but a mission was a mission. It must have been around six in the evening. The sun was still out, and because of the long summer days, nightfall wasn't till much later. I knew just by seeing them that they had had a rough day. The tall lady, who was the driver, had her left arm scorched by the sun. Both looked terribly sunburnt and tired. When we got to the parlor, they went straight to the matter.

The message was brief. They told me that God had set angels that took them straight to the preacher's house. First, there had been a family waiting to catch a bus and when they stopped to offer them a ride, it so happened that the family was precisely from the very same village and personally knew the preacher and his family. Then, to get to his house, they would have to cross a river, but the bridge was down. The ladies explained that God had "angels" waiting with a boat ready to help them cross the river and direct them straight to the preacher's sister's house. They wasted no time. Jane and Mary met with his sister, who told them he was in the United States, in Nebraska, and that he was getting married that upcoming weekend. His sister wasn't sure that he'd really go through with the wedding because he had stood up two brides in Mexico on different occasions. She told my angels that at both those occasions, he had not even shown up. Of course, she explained, this had happened when he was a teenager, and now, in his mid-thirties, he was probably ready to settle down and start a family.

Jane and Mary heard the story, learned of his upcoming nuptials, and immediately returned to Brownsville. After meeting with me and telling me the whole story, they told me that they were going to Nebraska, to his wedding. They assured me they would write to me and tell me if he had really gone through with the marriage this time. With that said, they excused themselves for being so sweaty and tired; they had to call it a night because they had to start off early (on Tuesday) for the state of Nebraska in order to make it to the wedding that weekend.

About a week later, I had a letter in the mail from God's messengers, with no return address. The note simply stated that they had attended the wedding ceremony and that my beloved preacher had indeed gotten married. That was it. Nothing else. It was then that the Holy Spirit showed me why God had not allowed us to even start a relationship. What if he had stood me up like he had done before? That would have killed me spiritually, and my anger at God would have deepened. Jesus had been my faithful friend since age nine, and I realized that He certainly would not allow anything destructive to happen to our relationship. Oh, how humiliated and ashamed I felt for having doubted my Lord and Savior, yet He had gone out of His way just for me!

It was then that my eyes were opened and I realized the Lord had sent these two angels to speak to me and, through them, learn that

His plans for my future were worth waiting for. To this day, I have never heard from Sister Mary or Sister Jane again. I'm sure they are somewhere in the world delivering another of God's messages for the purpose of healing another broken heart, as was mine.

CHAPTER 6

Wedding Bells

It had been a year and a half since I'd left Berea Bible Institute and I wasn't doing much other than helping out in my home church. This, I thought, would be my chance to go back to college in pursuit of my teaching degree. Come January 1977, as I prepared to register for the spring semester, the Reverend Vidal Garza, who had just started a Bible institute in his own church in Brownsville four months prior, insisted that I join him and the Reverend José Cervantes in establishing the school. I agreed and put off going to college to help with the Bible school. When Brother Garza learned of my contributions at Berea (1973–1975), he assigned me as the institute's administrator. We were now a team of three. Brother Garza was the president, Brother Cervantes the vice president, and I served as the administrator and secretary/treasurer. In addition to our responsibilities as executives, we also taught night courses once or twice a week, as did local pastors who assisted us.

The first school year (1976–1977) was a complete success, not only for the twelve students enrolled but also for the school itself, as it marked the beginning of Betel Bible Institute, later renamed Southmost Bible Institute, a Bible school that thrives till today. I enjoyed teaching at Bible school. I would have never dreamed it would become the means by which the Lord would cause a sudden shift in my life. Two years later, the reason surfaced. God had something else lined up for me: a husband, a daughter, and a new ministry, all in one big package.

With God's no during the summer of '76, who would even think of a boyfriend or of the possibility of marriage anymore? I didn't bother to pray about the issue. Marriage was totally out of my mind. Out of my mind, yes. But not out of God's.

The success of the second year of the Bible school would ultimately be overshadowed by tragedy. I was teaching that semester, but because I had given my final exam a week early, I was not at the school the night of the terrible news. On April 26, 1978, at around eleven thirty, my pastor (who was also a faculty member and happened to be at the school administering his last exam) called the staff to inform us that one of our students had just lost his wife and two of his three children in a car accident.

Mr. Reynaldo R. González had never taken his family to Bible school with him as he, like most students, had to rush to school after work. Even though most of our students were from the Brownsville area, some came from Raymondville, Harlingen, and San Benito, where he was from. None of us knew the family, but the devastating news sent shock waves through the school's faculty, staff, and students. Why him? He was such a humble, good, and quiet person. The only words I had ever heard him say were just, "God bless you," upon entering or exiting the classroom every Monday, Wednesday, and Friday.

I got up to let my mom and my sister Melva know about Pastor Amaya's call. Then I immediately went to my room and knelt by my bedside crying, hurting, and even questioning God. How could something so tragic happen to one of our students? I cried and prayed with a heavy heart. Then, totally out of context, incongruent with the sense of mourning I was feeling, a voice in my mind told me, "He's going to be your husband." I shook my head. Who on earth would be thinking of a husband at a time like this? I considered the thought diabolical and began rebuking it. I was angry at the voice. How dare this voice minimize my student's loss? The indignation I felt was palpable.

During the first funeral service, I found out that Reynaldo happened to be the brother of our good friends Ramiro, Raul, and Enedelia González. Students living in rural San Benito were bused to schools in the Los Fresnos school district—my hometown school district. Raul and Enedelia had been my sister Hilda's peers in grade school, and Ramiro had graduated with my sister Carmen. What a small world!

Mom and I attended the final service at the family's small church, which was jam-packed with mourners. Many people, including us, had to stand outside giving the very large González family the opportunity to be indoors where three caskets lay in front of the altar. The family's pastor, the Reverend José Luis González, no relation to the family, together with other local and district leaders, officiated in the funeral services. Mom and I did not go to the graveside service with the procession. We went back home with heavy hearts at witnessing such a painful sight.

Not once that summer, nor at the beginning of the fall when we went back to Bible school, did that terrible thought or "voice" cross my mind. I was plainly not interested in any relationship, and marriage was not even a desirable thought. I minded my own business, working days as a migrant schoolteacher aide and teaching nights at the Bible school.

Eight months later, I was shocked when my student, Reynaldo González, insulted me by calling me at home one night to invite me as his guest to the students' Christmas dinner. The student body was preparing the dinner and had suggested that all those married take their spouses and that singles take a guest.

How dare a student invite a professor! I was furious. That was a terrible insult. What did he think I was? So many ugly thoughts crossed my mind. Here I was, a "young" lady, now thirty-four and single, and this widower with whom I mourned the death of his family a few months earlier called me. Angrily and not being able to bear it anymore, I went over to Mom's room, and standing by her bed, I explained what had just happened. She shocked me too! The words that followed did not even sound like Mom was talking. It wasn't in her nature to take things or insults of this magnitude so calmly. All she told me was "Oh, stop fussing. He's the one." Now, for someone else to insult me was one thing, but for Mom? My very own mother? That was more than I could take! I stomped out of her room in disbelief and went straight to my room, got on my knees, and started crying my anger out till I could cry no more.

Before I knew it, my anger had turned into pity for my student, Brother Reynaldo. As I prayed, I remember trying to justify my anger and the feeling of being insulted. I explained to God that I didn't mean to be ugly to him when I refused to go as his guest. And it didn't mean that I felt a sense of superiority to him or that I felt he was not good enough for me. I felt so bad and ashamed for my reaction. I apologized to God but stood my ground: a student should not mingle with his professors, so I thought.

The Christmas holidays were over all too quick. Returning to work and to Bible school was a blessing. At Bible school, everything was back to normal. It didn't bother me to see Reynaldo, nor did he seem bothered to see me after my harsh response in December. He had shared his interest in me with a couple of his buddies in class (men about his age), and I later learned that they and others encouraged him to ask me out again. Some family members and two elderly ladies who were powerful prayer warriors were not only praying for him but also explained to him that a modest young lady was not going to respond positively on the first try; therefore, he must not give up if he really was interested and ready to move forward with his life.

Brother Reynaldo took the advice to heart and at the end of January called me up at home again to invite me out to have dinner on a Saturday evening. This time I was nice and polite, not hostile as before. The guilt trip I'd gone through before made me accept the invitation. There were a couple of conditions though. First, I would invite another couple to go with us. Second, I would drive myself to the restaurant instead of him picking me up, which Mom would not allow. Third, I had to be back home before ten o'clock. With Melva and me being the only two remaining siblings at home—Melva twenty-seven and me thirty-four—we still had to obey the rules.

I had never dated before and I blushed in embarrassment. The idea tortured me, but I couldn't hurt his feelings again. After all, he was such a meek person and I didn't want to be perceived as being prideful or that I felt too good for him.

I invited Rachel and Joel. Rachel was another one of my students who must have learned about his interest in me, because she had mentioned him to me once or twice before. They helped ease the tension. Reynaldo was so shy and nervous during our first date that after dinner, he discovered he'd left his keys in the ignition of his locked car. With the help of a restaurant guest, he and Joel worked at it until they opened the car. Poor guy. We all left, and I was so relieved.

A couple of days before Valentine's Day, he called me up for the third time. This time, he insisted on us going by ourselves, as he wanted to "talk" to me. I don't know why I accepted. Maybe I was easing into the possibility that Mom was right about him. That day turned out to be our first real date. There he asked my permission to court me. He explained that his interest in me was serious. He had prayed a lot for me, after he had lost his family, and he wanted to move on with his life for his and his daughter, Dina's, sake.

Was it really me? What was I doing? Why did I say yes to this courting business? And why was all this happening so fast? I didn't have time to answer all the questions in my mind. It was almost ten and I needed to get home quick. He must have left the happiest man on Earth that night, but I had another issue to take care of.

Before driving myself home, I had one stop to make. I stopped at a friend's house to drop off the Valentine's chocolate box Reynaldo had given me. I wouldn't dare go home with it. Some things never change. Remember my rings and watch dilemma eighteen years before? I gave my friend a quick explanation, left the box, and rushed home in a puzzled state. Then it hit me. It had to be the Lord's doing. There was no other explanation. It was clear to me that God was "making up" for having denied me the handsome Mexican preacher with another tall, handsome, God-fearing man who I was beginning to love.

In April of that year, Reynaldo proposed, and I accepted. But I had one very serious condition: that his daughter, Dina, would come live with us once we were married. Both he and his daughter were living with his dad and two older sisters. He assured me Dina would welcome me and happily accept my condition, because she was anxious to once more have a house of her own. Why was I saying all this or demanding so much? In a few months since officially beginning our relationship, I had come to love him in a different, serious, mature way. I did not feel sorry for him anymore. I could genuinely see myself as his wife, and he and Dina as my husband and daughter. I knew that I wasn't madly in love with him like I had been with my very first boyfriend when I was sixteen, not that I had prayed or cried over him like I had done for "my preacher" man. This relationship was different. It was as though I had skipped all the superficial, temporary romance and dived right into the deep end of a serious, true-love relationship. I just knew he was the man for me and that it was God's will. I remember telling God, "This is your doing, so now help me." And He did.

A month later, Reynaldo sent his pastor and a friend to talk to my mom and ask for my hand in marriage. (While proud Americans, our Mexican heritage compels certain traditions, of which this was one. By tradition, the groom does not ask for the hand in marriage himself but instead sends a messenger, usually friends of his parents, as intermediaries. I thought this tradition was beautiful and everyone else in my family had done it. I was not going to be the exception.) Days later, his dad and his two sisters came over for the "official" visit. (This is the second part of the tradition, if the first meeting goes well.) We set our wedding date for July 28, giving us two months to prepare for the big day. For the reader doing the math, that's eight months after the first call, six months after the second call, and five months from when we officially became a couple. Melva was excited that my wedding would fall on her birthday, and Mom didn't object in the least.

When I shared the news with my pastor and the church, they were all in awe. No one had ever known or heard of me dating or being courted by any gentleman, much less heard me talking of marriage. All they knew was that I was serving God wholeheartedly and nothing but church, church, church occupied my mind. The adults at church and my youth group were all excited, and without my even mentioning the word *wedding*, they began volunteering and offering to help. The children, on the other hand, cried. They did not like the idea of me leaving them and not being their Friday night's children's church leader anymore. I had to literally bribe them to get them to join in the happiness everyone else was feeling. First, I promised I'd continue with the Friday night's children's church till the end of the year, and second, I promised them I'd have a separate room (at my wedding reception) solely for them with a children's wedding cake—just for them. With that said, they too rejoiced.

The wedding date of July 28, 1979, came quickly, but God was in charge and I just followed His instructions. He took care of the littlest details, and at the end of the day, everyone was praising God and marveling at such a "perfect" wedding. Every *t* had been crossed, and every *i* had been dotted. We had over five hundred adults and exactly 104 children. The adults were amazed at the catering service and marveled at the sight of Georgeana, my little four-year-old niece dressed as a bride, with her own little groomsman, walking in front of me in the reception hall, honoring and representing the children of my home church.

Angels By The Roadside

My wedding day, 1979, with my little bride, Georgeana, representing the children of my church on that special day.

Not one of the 104 children got up from their place. The Lord had led me to have two sponsors at each table to assist them. If any needed to get up, he or she had to be escorted by an adult. What a wedding! Who, if not the Lord, would have guided such preparations?

After the wedding celebrations were over and the honeymoon trip realized, I turned to my new ministry: my new home. Now I had a husband and a daughter. Dina was a very nice fourteen-year-old who had accepted me really well. She was also very brave and chose not to talk about her mom or her siblings, though I'd mention them in trying to help her cope with the loss.

I loved Dina and had accepted her as from the Lord and felt responsible for her life and for her spiritual well-being. Her father was ill, but no one knew the real diagnosis. We attributed the illness to possible flashbacks of the accident and the unbearable pain of having lost his first wife and two beautiful children. Because of his meekness and illness, he practically turned Dina over to me. Both her parents had been Christians and she'd been raised in the church, but the loss had been immense and she would need a lot of love, understanding, and counseling. It was a huge task, but I trusted that God would help me guide her in His path.

CHAPTER 7

Me, a Pastor?

A month to the day after we'd been married, my husband and I were offered a pastorate position in Olmito. Olmito is a very small community located between San Benito and Brownsville in deep South Texas. There was already a small mission holding services there, but it needed dedicated leadership. The "mission" had been under the auspices of Reynaldo's Assemblies of God home church. After negotiating and clarifying very important issues with his pastor, we accepted the position being offered.

The Assemblies of God sectional and district leaders were well informed that I would be the official senior pastor, while my husband's name, due to his illness, would only appear on paper as a titular pastor. Reynaldo, having only recently graduated from Bible school (where we met), had no ministerial background and thus relied on my many years of experience in various fields within ministry. He accepted the challenge to act as a "title" pastor, meaning that he would carry the title, but ultimately I'd be preaching, teaching, and handling all the church businesses as required by our state laws and the bylaws of the General Council of the Assemblies of God.

We started the mission with only two families (four adults and two children). The Martinez and the Perez families were the only official members. They too understood that I was the pastor and anything and everything related to the church had to be addressed to me and ultimately approved by me. The church members were never to bother my husband or expect anything or any kind of participation from him. They all knew he was ill.

Week after week, service after service, we'd see newcomers join the fold. God began to bless the tiny mission in a mighty way. In a month's time, we had the men's, women's, and youth departments running. Sunday school was overcrowded in the little building we were using. The youth and children's classes were held under a tree shade or in an old school bus that had been repurposed to accommodate additional classes.

Four months had gone by, and though we were working hard at church, we were also preparing for Dina's fifteenth birthday party. (The typical Mexican-culture-inspired party for a fifteen-year-old girl is called a "quinceñera." It is a big deal for the girl and her family; preparations often resemble those of a small wedding.) This had been her mother's wish, and the least we could do was to honor that wish. The celebration was great, and Dina looked beautiful. Just seeing her smile, laugh, and play again was a sign of healing and that our prayers for her were being answered.

Dina at her quinceñera, only four months after my wedding.

It hadn't been easy for Dina to transfer from her home church to Olmito, but there is no doubt that it had been a blessing in disguise because she needed a change of venue. At her home church, she'd have the vivid picture in her mind of the three caskets which had once lain there, and of all the funeral services. Surely, God knew how this would affect her and prepared her for a change: new challenges and a new place of worship at the Olmito church.

That little mission, named Templo El Divino Rey (translated, it means "the Divine King Church"), seemed like a beacon for the residents in the Olmito area. The good news traveled fast. God was moving in a mighty way and filling up the little church building with people from the nearby communities. Reynaldo, Dina, and I rejoiced and continued to work to the best of our ability.

The Lord blessed us in such a miraculous way. Eighteen months later, we were closing the deal on a new property and starting to build a new church in a more centralized section of the community. Many Christian friends came to aid in the building project. Every single person of the church was taking part. I mean all of the men, women, youths, and children were helping, hands on, in some form. Everyone worked as one until the task was over.

By this time, my husband's illness had worsened and I had become emotionally distressed. He had just been diagnosed with MS, and as a consequence, with his gait beginning to be affected, he was unable to keep his job of twenty-five years with Zales Jewelers. He loved being at church, helping out in what little he could, so we continued pastoring the Olmito church for five and a half years. During these years, our family grew by two. Rey Jr. was born in 1980 and Mike was born in 1981.

Pastoring this thriving Christian community was such a joy, despite the fact that my husband's illness was beginning to demand more of my attention. I was shocked, therefore, when without any reason apparent to me at the time, I was instructed by God to leave the church. We had just finished an ambitious building project. I had just presided over perhaps the most notable church-planting attempt in Olmito. The struggle with tending to my husband, daughter, and the church was taxing, but not impossible. While I did not understand it, I did not resist God's instructions. I knew they were His instructions. Surely He had other plans—plans that would alleviate the burden and give me time to tend to my husband, to Dina, and to my two young boys.

The church families had been very helpful and loved my kids dearly. Rey Jr. had just turned four and Mike was two months shy of his third birthday when, at a members meeting, I broke the news of my resignation. I helped the church by staying and guiding the members through the process of selecting and electing a replacement pastor. It took a while, but I was officially out in August 1984.

A Spiritual Shift

Leaving the church in Olmito was heartbreaking. My husband, Dina, and the boys were taking it real hard. I almost regretted having obeyed God. I felt physically weak and felt I had reached the end of the rope both emotionally and spiritually. After battling the greatest turmoil of my life, I sought counseling from an experienced minister who knew me since childhood. The Reverend Dr. Roberto Avitia from Brownsville advised me and prayed for me with such an assurance that the Lord would "open a new door" for me real soon because it was obvious that I needed to be, as he said, "behind the pulpit" ministering somewhere. He encouraged me by declaring into my life that I would soon recover from all the emotional stress and be renewed physically as well.

Exactly two weeks after Reverend Avitia had prayed for me, Mr. and Mrs. Santiago Resendez came knocking at my door, pleading for me to go help them in a small mission (church) they had started two or three years prior at their home. They shared with me the struggles they had endured as they, without any training in ministry, were simply following God's call to begin a mission. They admitted they were getting ready to shut down when they heard that I was no longer pastoring in Olmito. They (a small group of sixteen people, mostly relatives) had prayed for

God to send someone to oversee the group. They had decided that if God did not send them a pastor, they would know it was His will that each should go their separate ways and look for other churches to attend. I agreed to go talk to them the following Sunday to explain all that "taking over" a mission or church entailed. I also explained my position as a minister of the Assemblies of God and that if they wanted me to pastor the church, they would no longer be an independent group but rather a mission affiliated with the Assemblies of God.

It turns out that that was precisely what they wanted to hear. The group was tired of having independent ministers or speakers come for a month or two and then leave them like a flock of sheep without a shepherd. After discussing among themselves all the advantages and obligations in having a dedicated pastor, the group agreed to my terms and we were officially installed as pastors of the small mission on February 17, 1985. To officially belong to the Assemblies of God, we applied and filled out all the required paperwork and ultimately registered the church with its new name: Templo Ebenezer Asambleas de Dios (translated as "Ebenezer Assembly of God Church").

Even though it was a new church, because Ebenezer was operating well with all the required departments and was financially sound, we were soon recognized as a district-affiliated church. We continued having services at the mission (at the Resendez residence) for about a year. Even though we had added a few feet to expand the size of the meeting room, the place filled to capacity in every church service. We definitely needed a new place. The need to relocate was urgent. By the end of our second year at Ebenezer, we had already purchased a new property (four lots) and had begun the construction of a new church building. What great things God had done for us. He had taken us out of Olmito to plant a church in San Benito.

August 22, 1987, would be a day to remember and celebrate. We had people from far and near, together with dozens of ministers, come to the inauguration of the new church building the Lord had given us. Our district leaders were amazed as they witnessed how the Lord had blessed and brought us through in just two and a half years. The hardships of the building process were over and we felt ready for the new challenges ahead. We rejoiced with extreme gratitude for having a "real church," God's own house of worship and a beautiful and humble group of people who loved the Lord. What a difference, what a spiritual shift pastoring had been from the type of ministry I had been involved with before marriage. The Olmito church-planting experience would be in our lives forever. Ebenezer now had all our attention.

Photo of the church-building project completed in Olmito, Texas. The church was named Templo El Divino Rey Asambleas De Dios, a name it retains to this day.

Photo of Templo Ebenezer Asambleas De Dios in San Benito, Texas, as it appears in 2015. The main sanctuary was built in 1987. The Sunday school annex, the separate building to the left of the main sanctuary, was built in 2000.

A New Revelation

With a brand-new church building, we wanted to start purchasing some appliances and other needed items. With that in mind, someone donated an old refrigerator, and frankly, I was perturbed. That person had taken out of her house an old, rusty refrigerator and had replaced it with a new one, donating the old one to the church. Sister Elva, our church secretary, could see how disturbed I was, but she said nothing. Little did I know that my attitude toward that particular donation would be the reason for seriously hurt feelings and that a brand-new experience in ministry would arise from that old refrigerator.

Not a soul knew why Sister Elva fell into a state of depression right before our eyes. Her mom and sisters, also members of the church, were concerned for her, but when asked if she would share her problems, tears rolled down her cheeks and with a red-blushed face she would just say, "Don't worry. It's okay." We—her family and I—knew things weren't okay, because she had never acted this way before. As her pastor, it hurt me to see her withdrawing from all conversations, turning away with tears and keeping whatever troubled her to herself. I prayed earnestly.

I sobbed as I asked the Lord to help her. I didn't have the slightest idea what her problem was, but it had to be a serious one; otherwise, she would have told someone in the church and would have requested prayer from someone by now. Little did I know that I, her pastor, was the problem. Here I was innocently praying for her, not knowing I had caused the wound in her heart that now manifested so clearly to everyone around her.

The issue had been that when Sister Elva had asked me to meet her at church to show me the donated refrigerator, I hadn't necessarily picked my words carefully to express my feelings of disgust and disappointment. I plain rejected the idea of keeping it, though we couldn't afford one just then. She just listened, never said a word or demonstrated any kind of hurt, and even seemed to agree with me. With nothing else to discuss, we locked up the building and each went our separate ways.

Me, a Pastor?

From that moment on, Sister Elva's attitude changed drastically and all she did was cry. As for me, I wept all the way home and knelt while pouring out my heart, asking myself how anyone would dare give secondhand items to God when He deserved the best.

Oh, how we loved our new church. My family and I didn't mind spending hours cleaning and beautifying the premises. It was on one of those days when we'd just come home from cleaning that a miracle happened.

My husband and I had just returned home from church, where we'd been sweeping and cleaning up for Sunday services. Physically ill and exhausted, my husband threw himself on the bed to rest before showering. My boys, ages six and seven, were tired from the summer heat and ready for a nap. No sooner had I lain down to rest when the Lord called out to me, "Get up, and go to church." Without thinking, I snapped back, out loud, "But Lord, we just came from church!"

His gentle yet direct instructions came back to me again with the same words: "Get up, and go to church." This time, I got on my feet, went to my husband, and quietly, as to not wake the boys, whispered to him, "I'll be right back. I have to go to church. I'll tell you when I come back."

Once there, I walked throughout the sanctuary and the adjacent kitchen and dining area. I looked and listened, looked and listened, but I did not hear or see anything. I walked around the place again for the second or third time while looking for something that the Lord might want to point out, but again there was nothing in sight. Bewildered, I returned home. On the way home, I explained to God that I hadn't seen *anything*.

As soon as I got home, I jumped into the shower before my husband or kids would wake up. I prayed as I showered, speaking to God aloud, and somewhat puzzled, I repeated the phrase "But I didn't see anything. But I didn't see anything." Then, like a flash, there it was! "You didn't see anything! You didn't see the refrigerator!" It was like an echo sounding loudly in my heart and ears. "You didn't see the refrigerator." It never occurred to me to look for anything in particular, and I wasn't thinking of Sister Elva or the refrigerator when we'd gone to clean up or even the second time when I'd returned upon the Lord's request.

Faster than words can explain, I got out of the shower and called Sister Elva to meet me at church immediately. Without hesitation, she replied she would be there. I wasn't about to ask her a single question or mention the refrigerator. I didn't need to. It was all clear to me now. The Lord had just revealed to me the reason for her depression, her tears, and her change of attitude.

I did not go to the kitchen to verify and see if the refrigerator was there or not. The Lord had told me it wasn't and that was that. We both entered the sanctuary and I asked her to sit in the very first pew as I stood in front of her. I relayed the whole story and God's revelation. I cried as I repeatedly apologized for my abrupt reaction the day she had shown me the old appliance. I was so sorry for having caused her so much pain. Sister Elva finally, between sobs, though she was a tough, strong woman, confessed to being so hurt that she had had the refrigerator removed that same day. She had gotten hurt because a non-Christian acquaintance had donated the item and though she too would have preferred a new one, she couldn't refuse accepting it. In any case, after apologizing and reconciling, we prayed together and put the matter behind us.

What an experience for our church secretary. She knew, without a shadow of a doubt, that it had been God and God alone who had revealed the matter to me, because no one else knew what had happened two weeks prior. By the time she left, she was herself again.

To experienced leaders, whether in ministry or other professions, Sister Elva's issue may seem like just another issue from just another member, but this was different. To begin with, Sister Elva was not the baby-business, sensitive type. She was a solid Christian woman who wanted to please her God and her pastor and found herself torn between the two. Here, real pain was perceived by me in someone I loved. That pain was not only affecting her but all those she loved. Pastoring, a profession that deals as much with administering an organization as in any other profession, is different in that it also deals with hearts. That day, God mended Sister Elva's heart and taught me another important lesson on pastoring: choose words more carefully.

As for me, before I returned home, I went to the very space where the whole issue had begun—where the refrigerator had once stood. There, I poured my heart out to the Lord. I praised Him for Sister Elva, who was indeed a true committed Christian and an excellent secretary. I praised God for answering our prayers on her behalf, and above all, I praised God for His powerful revelation that cured all the hurt and gave us peace and joy once more.

What an experience! The God that had saved me was still manifesting Himself to me even though many years had gone by since the very first revelation when I was just nine years old. Praise the Almighty!

CHAPTER 8

Healing Wings

The year 1990 was a difficult for me. I started the year with a project in mind, hoping to complete it by my birthday that year. The project was to compile 150 old-fashioned Christian songs and make a new hymnal. Unfortunately, I had to put the project on hold due to a sudden illness that struck me and lasted for about six and a half months. I had been on a leave of absence from school since mid-November and through the Christmas break due to hoarseness. I felt better and returned to work in January to heed to the doctors' constant advice for me to reduce my talking time. How could I possibly teach, preach, or sing without using my vocal chords?

This was much more serious than I thought, and I was scared to go to the doctors, lest they diagnose me with cancer. Cancer had taken the lives of my father and several other Silva family members. I dreaded to hear the word, not that I was scared to die but I felt for my boys who were still very young—nine and ten. And what would Dina do with her bed-bound dad and two kid brothers? She was just a sweet twenty-five year old. The thought depressed me, but I had to shove it off and be brave for them all, and for my church.

With ulcers on both sides of my tongue and a burning sensation in my mouth and throat that water could no longer soothe, I decided to go to a throat specialist. He immediately diagnosed me with a tumor on my vocal chords and advised immediate attention and rest. He also recommended for me to stop talking and placed me on a leave of absence from school again. That gave me time to go to other doctors for a second opinion. Three of the five specialists I went to said the very same thing, but fear kept me going for one more opinion.

I was diagnosed with several incurable diseases, including lupus. Ultimately, a new physician at the Diagnostic Clinic in Harlingen, Texas, diagnosed me with Sjogren's syndrome, also known as Mikulicz disease and Sicca syndrome, an autoimmune disease in which my own immune cells attacked and destroyed the glands that produce tears and saliva. He didn't mention the tumor at all but explained that the dryness was the reason for the severe burning sensation in my throat and insisted that the treatment was to fill the glands with artificial saliva, artificial tears, and artificial mucus. This would not cure the disease but would relieve the dryness and burning sensation.

"Relief? I don't need artificial anything," I told myself. "I need God!" I needed a host of angels with healing wings to comfort me in this time of need. I felt so lonely and sick and needed physical and spiritual healing. There was absolutely no one I could share my problem with. Mom would become dead worried if I told her the diagnosis, and I was afraid to announce it to my congregation, lest it would affect their faith.

Not accepting any artificial fillings of any kind, I decided to go back to the very first physician I'd seen. He immediately gave me the orders for admission to the hospital for surgery, as the tumor (he had initially mentioned) had grown somewhat in a month's time. That was on a Friday in the month of May in 1990. I was scheduled to undergo surgery the following Monday. How I thank God that Sundays come before Mondays. That meant that the church would have a chance to pray for me before the surgery.

Come Sunday, I announced to the church my having to report to the hospital first thing in the morning for surgery. Everyone had suffered with me just by seeing what I was going through, and the sudden announcement of my having to undergo surgery impacted the already emotional congregation. The speaker I had for that night alleviated the pain when he called everyone to the altar to come pray for me. They all prayed with great fervor and faith, asking God to heal their pastor.

I couldn't sleep that Sunday night after the evening service. I fell to my knees before the Great Physician. I took the hospital orders I needed to present the following morning and lifted them up, showing them to my Friend and eternal Companion. I showed the paper to the One that had saved me at age nine and who had been with me in tougher and more difficult times during my many years of journeying with Him. I cried out to Jesus, "I have never known you to need a laser to do surgery, and besides, I am not going to just drop your people's prayers. So in Your name, I tear this paper and will go to sleep, and you take care of the rest."

I woke up completely healed! Halleluiah! Glory to God! I could talk pain free, without any burning sensations, and no more needed a water bottle at hand to sooth my throat. I could speak and sing! I would be able to teach and preach and resume my responsibilities at church. For six and a half months, I had invited different speakers to preach on Sunday nights. The lay ministers and department heads would help out with the midweek services. And now that I was totally healed, I'd give my testimony everywhere I'd go, and it would certainly be written in the hymnal I still intended to compile. That project that began in 1990 finally materialized in 1995, and every person who now sings from my hymnal bears witness of God's healing power.

Healing Wings

A photograph of the hymnal *Cantos Especiales,* which I compiled, containing 150 Spanish hymns, many of which I feared would have been lost forever if not preserved for future generations.

Things went back to normal. I went back to work as an elementary schoolteacher, just in time for the end-of-the-year duties. My sons would be out for the summer, and neither one had forgotten the promise of taking them to Disneyland when Rey would turn ten. His tenth birthday had come and gone, but I had been too sick to even think about a trip away from home, and now that I was healed, I had to keep my promise. We all had gone through so much during those six to eight months that we deserved a real vacation. With great joy and praises to God, we prepared for the long-due family outing, the fourteen-day vacation referred to and detailed in chapter 1.

Leave Ebenezer?

God had continued blessing our church. No more fundraisers, no more building projects to take care of. By this time, all the work and stress of leading at church, at home, and at work was taking its toll on me. I was really exhausted trying to tend to the church, keep my full time job as an elementary schoolteacher, teaching at Bible school once or twice a week, and tending to my family. My husband's health got worse, and in the midst of all the work, I had to make frequent trips to the Methodist Hospital in Houston so that he could receive treatment for the rapidly advancing MS.

The year 1991 was for major decisions. Though I kept busy and going full force, I felt that my life had fallen into a rut. I'd been so very busy with church that I had, to a certain degree, neglected my husband, Dina, and my growing boys. I started feeling sorry for myself and for my family. I felt alone and annoyed by the littlest things anyone at church would say or do. I had come to the end of the proverbial road physically, emotionally, and spiritually. I needed help from above and needed it desperately. Oh, how I prayed for divine intervention. Were there any angels available to assist me now? Would God talk to me and guide me as He had before? All I knew was that I couldn't take it anymore, and I wanted to go away with my family and be left alone so that I'd enjoy them and make up for the lost time.

One option was to resign as pastor, but I didn't want to make an abrupt decision or leave without God's approval. Besides, where could I go with a sick, bed-bound husband and two youngsters? By this time, Dina had graduated from high school, was employed at a department store, and could not go with us regardless of where we went. If we did go away for some time off, she would have to stay at the González's farm with her aunts, Tina and Carmen.

The Lord began compelling me to take time off from Ebenezer and move to Dallas. He even gave me the name of the retired minister that would come and fill in for me while I was away. Day after day, night after night, the Lord would reveal to me the minister's name. He had been my husband's pastor when Reynaldo was only a youngster. The Reverend Reymundo Hernandez had visited us once before but had left immediately after the service to make it to the airport in time to catch his flight, so we didn't get to talk much at all. I didn't know the man personally. I didn't even know if he was currently on staff at a church or not. All I knew was that he lived in San Angelo, Texas.

It all happened so fast. I was still working, so wherever we would want to move, the move would have to be during the summer months.

Around the middle of May, right after a Sunday school class, the Lord's call hit me like a ton of bricks. My heart's palpitation was abnormal. I was ready to break down and could not contain my tears.

In desperation, I asked Dina to take the kids out for lunch somewhere. I explained that I needed to talk to her dad. With those words, and noticing the tears on my face, she looked at me as if she were seeing a ghost and asked, "Why? What did the Lord tell you?" I promised I'd explain later but that she needed to leave quickly.

My husband had been in a semicoma for so long and didn't know about himself or his surroundings, and I certainly didn't share my problems or frustrations with him. What for? He wouldn't understand a thing I'd say, and besides, he was asleep or sedated (due to the large number of medications he was on) most of the time. My heart was aching, and all I wanted to do was pray and cry my heart out.

When Dina and the kids left, I went to my room and threw myself on my knees. I wept before my loving Father. After praying for a while and understanding as clear as day what God wanted me to do, I went to my husband's bedside, where he lay sound asleep, shook him, and woke him up. He opened his eyes for a few minutes, long enough for me to tell him, "Babe (as I always called him), we're moving to Dallas."

As soon as he heard those words, he sat up and asked with great concern, "Who are you going to leave at church?"

"Me? Not Me," I replied. "The Lord is sending Brother Reymundo Hernandez of San Angelo to come and substitute."

Two seconds later, he was sound asleep. I wasn't even sure he'd heard me. I positioned him comfortably back in his hospital bed and returned to my room where I broke down like never before. I cried so hard and loud that I even buried my face in my pillow as to not to be heard by Dina or the kids, should they return without me noticing.

When I finally got a hold of myself, I got up, went to the phone, and called Brother Hernandez. After a couple of tries, a man answered. It was Brother Hernandez. When he identified himself, I explained who I was. He asked for my husband. I did not answer his question but instead asked him, "Brother, has God asked you to come to San Benito?" I explained that we were moving to Dallas temporarily and that God had spoken to me, giving me his name as the indicated person to come substitute for me. My question had been so direct and so unexpected that he was caught off guard. He later explained that he didn't know what to say but knew that this was coming directly from God. As it turns out, the Lord had, precisely the night before, been speaking with him, beckoning him to get out and preach. He had been in isolation for a long time, mourning the death of one of his sons. God had to literally get him out of his room. After a brief pause, all he said was that he would talk to his wife and would have a response for me the following day. He said he'd call me at 6:00 p.m. on Monday.

Pastor Hernandez did not say yes or no about coming, yet because I trusted God, I got off the phone feeling certain that he was coming. With a sigh of relief, a sense of assurance came over me and I started praising God, thanking Him for a done deal. When Dina and the boys returned, I shared with them all that God had been doing and the plans of moving to Dallas sometime in the summer.

Dina was glad we were getting away for a while—for her dad's sake. She'd have to stay behind, due to her job, but was content with knowing we'd get a deserved break. The boys became very excited. No doubt they, too, had been suffering quietly. Just weeks before, they had asked if I could stop being a pastor and give up the church. They were growing up so fast and, while never demanding, needed so much more attention than I had been able to give them.

The idea of moving to Dallas was received with joy by the boys. Both having completed another school year, passing with flying colors, the prospect of returning to school with an extraordinary summer experience would add to the trip's excitement. Rey was a fifth grader and Mike a nine-year-old in the third grade.

Pastor Hernandez had not confirmed his coming to San Benito, but I still called my presbyter, the Reverend Juan Trevino, on Monday during my lunch break and asked to meet with him at his church office at three thirty that afternoon. I explained it was urgent, and he agreed. Right after school, I rushed to Brownsville to Brother Trevino's office to inform him that I was taking a leave of absence from the church and that Pastor Hernandez was coming to fill in for me while I was gone. I shared all the details about how God had dealt with me—my call to Brother Hernandez the day before and how he was supposed to call me that same afternoon at six o'clock to confirm or turn down the invitation. Because I was so sure that this was all God's doing, I spoke with such assurance and boldly claimed it as a done deal. When Brother Trevino learned that his old-time friend from San Angelo was the Lord's choice to come and aid me, he was so astonished that all he could do was repeatedly say, "This has got to be from God." He burst into tears and started praying for me and praising God for revealing His will in such glorious manifestations. Somehow, he also felt that Brother Hernandez would call me that evening with an affirmative response.

By the time six o'clock came around that afternoon, I knew exactly what Pastor Hernandez's response was going to be. God had already set it in my heart. Sure enough, during the phone call, which began precisely at 6:00 p.m. as scheduled, all the pastor said was that he had spoken to his wife the night before and as they prayed together about the issue, the Lord instructed them to come and tend to Ebenezer "until He would heal" me.

I don't know what the congregation saw in me, but when I called a members meeting to explain every last detail of what had been going on in my life and how God had spoken to me, they knew this action was entirely from God. They knew this was not the first time God had spoken to me or revealed something as great as this. After all, I had often testified and shared experiences I had had with the Lord since childhood. They knew about God's visitations through His celestial beings and how angels would practically take me by the hand and guide me to higher grounds or to peaceful valleys as the one He was about to take me to.

By the time the Hernandez arrived in San Benito in mid- June, we were ready to go. Everything was in place for our arrival in Dallas. My husband's sister and family were eagerly waiting for us. They had just bought a house for the purpose of renting it and wanted us to be the first ones there to, "bless it." The Lord took care of the moving details, including everything my husband needed, from a hospital bed to home health nurses and the like. There was not a single thing that we had back home that the Lord had not already supplied for us in our new house. And because God loves the little children, He made sure my boys had plenty of toys and entertainment activities squared away for them, even upon our arrival. How great God really is.

The healing process had begun just with the thought of moving away. All the excitement of going on an extended vacation had filled our hearts. The farewells were painful, especially leaving Dina and the church families behind, but we would soon be back.

Even though our stay in Dallas was only for a month and a half, God's grace and mighty hand healed me completely. He had healed me physically, mentally, emotionally, and spiritually. The boys had been touched in a miraculous way too. They were overjoyed when they learned we were going back home and back to our very own church. Both were thrilled when I explained that Pastor Hernandez and his wife would be going back to San Angelo as soon as we'd get home. They were thankful that I had not resigned, and that meant Mom would still be pastor at Ebenezer. It also meant that they could continue having the same PK (pastor's kids) privileges as before. They could continue being the church musicians and have a master key to open and close the church buildings during service days. It even meant they could continue sitting in the front pew beside Dad's wheelchair. Rey once came to me just to say, "Mom, I'm a PK, and once a PK, forever a PK." Mike nodded, seconding those words.

That said it all. It was clear that coming back to Ebenezer was a family decision.

My husband was doing better. He had somehow snapped out of the semicoma state he was in and was somewhat more alert to enjoy his daughter, his sons, and me. We were all a very happy family again, praise God.

We returned home on August 11, 1991. The whole church welcomed us with such sincere joy that words cannot explain. Reverend Hernandez preached his last sermon that night, and he and his wife didn't even wait for the morning to begin the return trip to San Angelo. At about 3:00 p.m. the next day, they called to let us know they had begun driving early and were already home. What a blessing they had been to Ebenezer. The church treasured their sermons, their songs, and their home visits and had befriended them dearly. They would be missed, but they were again back with their family—and we were with ours.

CHAPTER 9
A Dark Cloud

A dark cloud of mixed emotions came over my life when the Lord decided to "snatch" my mom ("Amá," as we all called her) from my side and into her heavenly home on June 17, 1995. So many people had come to pray for her, yet our prayers had apparently gone unanswered. After fourteen days in the hospital, and with evident signs that it was her time to go, she passed away as a triumphant Christian. I say she was snatched from me because of the feeling of having something so drastically and catastrophically torn from my life which her passing brought about.

I mourned my mom, my faithful angel, for eight months until that day, on February 17, 1996, when God healed my wound with His Word.

Every waking moment of every day during those eight months, I'd ask the Lord why He had not healed Mom. Day after day, I felt God had failed me by not answering my plea. That early February morning, as I was washing up, standing in front of the mirror, my daily routine of questioning God began. "Why Lord? Why couldn't you have given her a second chance? She went to the hospital trusting in your healing power. Why didn't you honor her?" It was as if I wanted to get back at God by pointing out to Him how much I was hurting because He had failed me, failed Mom's family and failed all nine of us.

While this questioning had become my morning routine, something different happened on that February morning. When I prayed the words

A Dark Cloud

"second chance," the Holy Spirit, as if emerging from the mirror and staring steadfast into my face, asked me, "How do you know how she was going to die if given a second chance?"

That poignant question took me back to the time when her gas water heater almost exploded in her face when she was investigating an odd smell one evening. Then I thought of the time that I thought someone had broken into her house and was torturing her.

A few years before, I had been terrified one early morning when my phone rang at 2:00 a.m. No one responded to my answer, but I heard what sounded like a moan as from someone in pain. The moan sounded just like Mom's voice. It sounded like someone was hurting her and putting her on the phone for me to hear and then hung up. I called her. She didn't answer. Trembling from head to toe, I managed to call the police in Brownsville, only to be get a voicemail recording. I called my local police station and was told to call Brownsville again. By that time, I was in a panicked state and was getting ready to get in my car and drive to Brownsville when I decided to call Mom's house once more. Lo and behold, she answered the phone. Ten dreadful minutes had passed since the first phone call. She sounded so peaceful. I burst out crying and told her what had happened. She scolded me, reminding me that that was precisely how the Devil attacked us at night, sometimes even in our sleep. After she had assured and reassured me that everything was okay, with a stern voice, she told me to pray it off and go to sleep. These memories flashed in my mind as I stood in front of my mirror. This was not how my daily complaints had gone before.

I started apologizing to the Holy Spirit. Trying to muff my voice from a scream, I began to thank Him that Mom hadn't died in a fire and that no one had ever entered her house, where she lived all alone, to hurt her. In the midst of my tears and uncontainable sobbing, I continued thanking God that she had never had to suffer the loss of a limb as many diabetic friends had. I was grateful she had never been diagnosed with cancer. I began to thank the Lord that she was never bed ridden or that she did not suffer a slow, painful death. So many things could have happened, yet God had been merciful and had taken her peacefully and quickly.

The Lord put an end to my daily interrogatories that February morning. I went to my room, grabbed my Bible, and knelt beside my bed. With a river of tears upon my face, I opened my Bible. Without looking for a specific Scripture passage, the Bible opened to the book of Isaiah. The Lord focused my eyes to chapter 57, verses 1 and 2. How much clearer could God be? How else could He tell me that He had taken her from the anguish and painful days ahead? How else could He show the love He had for Amá, the beloved Sister Caraveo as everyone knew her?

That was the end of my mourning period. Mom would live forever in my heart, and I knew she was, by far, better off in her heavenly home than in her earthly one. We miss her very much, but I know, without a shadow of a doubt, that my family and I will see her again someday.

Swords of Fire

After Mom went home to be with the Lord, Anita, my sister, went bankrupt, losing both her house and business. She came to live with us temporarily because I had rented Mom's house and it was not immediately available for her to use. While living with me, she witnessed a scary situation where God sent a host of angels to protect me from an intruder.

At who or at what were the dogs so fiercely barking and dashing to attack? Was it a ghost that they were seeing or a person trying to trespass onto our backyard?

It was around midnight. The night was pitch dark. My sister and I were awakened by the unusual behavior of her dog, Princess, who pulled to the end of the chain she was tethered to with such force that we were afraid she'd break the leash or injure herself. Our neighbor's dog dashed in the same direction as if attacking ferociously at something behind the brush right on the boundary line that separated our yard from an old log cabin behind our backyard. Both animals would run and then retreat with a scared whimper. Anita and I were peeking through the patio glass door but saw nothing. The dogs continued in their rage. My sister wanted to go out to calm Princess down, but I didn't let her. Instead, I started praying and rebuking.

My sister, Anita, with her beloved pet Siberian husky, Princess.

As I called on the Lord to cast out of our backyard whoever or whatever was trying to penetrate, a chill through my spine, goose bumps on my arms, and a ring of numbness around my mouth made me realize that I (not Anita) was under a spiritual attack.

I could sense that someone was hiding in the brush. Instantly, the Holy Spirit revealed to me who that person was. It was a man whom I had refused to baptize. He had stormed out of the church, directing his anger at me instead of at his sin that prevented him from being baptized.

As a pastor, I stood my ground, citing that baptisms were sacred and that he truly was not ready yet. But what was he doing there at this time of the night, and what were his intentions? Whatever they were, the Lord would take care of it all.

The dogs finally quieted down and my sister and I went back to sleep. About an hour later, the dogs' barking began again, and both of us jumped to our feet and back to the patio door. The dogs were more aggressive than before. This time, there were no chills or goose bumps, but as I prayed and rebuked, I literally saw angels with swords of fire standing along my property line. Although Anita could not see them, I saw angels positioned side by side, swinging their swords (crisscrossing the blades as the angels lifted and lowered them) to block whatever was still trying to cross into our backyard. The angels had the battlefront covered from ground to shoulder height. It must have been just a few seconds, but whatever had been there had been cast away. The dogs retreated with a whimper again and everything seemed to die out. I wasn't scared anymore; instead, I felt an overwhelming peace and a sense of security. We could finally go back to bed.

My sleep was so sound that at about 2:00 a.m., the dogs started barking again, but not in a rage like before. My sister told me the following morning that both she and our neighbor had gone outside to check on their dogs. Anita untangled Princess's chain and patted the calmed animal, while the neighbor, who was holding her dog, praised the animals for keeping watch through the night. After chatting for a while, each went back in to catch up on their sleep. That was the end of the dogs' commotion. The tempest was over. In the morning, I shared with my sister and family about the swords of fire in the angels' hands. What a scene!

To my surprise, a month later the gentleman came to my house and humbly apologized for his abrupt reaction to my refusal to baptize him a month earlier. He admitted that he had been so angry that he approached my house one late night with every intention to harm me physically.

"Something stopped me," he said.

I didn't tell him what I had seen, but as he spoke, I thanked the Lord for His protection. Psalm 34:7 says, "The angel of the Lord encamps around those who fear Him, and He delivers them." What a blessed promise!

Angels to the Rescue

In the months after Mom's passing, I admit that my focus had shifted away from church and onto my deep mourning. The sorrow and pain which consumed my every waking moment were gone after that encounter with God in February 1996. It was time to focus on church.

My family and the church worked diligently, almost nonstop, for the following eighteen months. There was always something to do, and everyone could see God moving in a mighty way. Our Sunday school attendance had doubled, our classrooms were overcrowded, and we needed to expand. *Expand* meant we needed new Sunday school facilities. So by midyear in 1998, we had all the building plans squared away with the city of San Benito for our new education building. We were ready to build again.

The project started very well. All the city and county requirements were met, and with money in hand, the project began. Little did we know that down the road, as in the days of Ezra, Haggai, and Zechariah in the Bible, the Enemy of God would set traps and use different people and a variety of problems to stall the progress of the building project for a year and a half.

The day came when I couldn't take it any longer. I cried till tears went dry, asking for God's intervention. After much prayer, the Lord finally sent His angels to the rescue. His first instructions to me were to get rid of all outsiders that had participated in the initial work and for us, the church, to take charge and complete the project. He would equip the men of the church with wisdom and would help them take care of even the smallest details. The Haggais and the Zechariahs would stand firm in the Word and encourage each other until the work would be totally done.

May God continue to bless the men and women who helped finish the project for their labor of love. Excitement was in the air as we saw the education building completed.

On Father's Day of the year 2000, we—the entire Ebenezer congregation, together with our sectional church leaders—gathered in front of the new building for its official dedication ceremony. What a day of victory! Every moment of desperation and all the trials we had overcome made our celebration even more meaningful. Our church children and youth, who had toiled with us during the bad times, were now ready to enjoy the good times in their brand-new classrooms.

A New Opened Door

I went about my business at home and at church. The next great events were my sons' high school graduations. Rey graduated in 1998, and by the second summer session, he was starting his college life at none other than Baylor University in Waco. Two years later, in 2000, Mike graduated and immediately headed to Southern Methodist University in Dallas to start the first summer session. Neither Rey nor Mike waited until the fall to begin college. They were both ambitious and ready to begin their studies. On both occasions, Dina accompanied my husband and me to go see the boys settled in the dorms and attend orientation. Leaving them behind was painful. I cried most of the way home both times. Dina couldn't help crying either. Her dad always kept his composure, staying strong for both of us ladies.

Mike had some unpleasant experiences at SMU from day one, especially at the dorm with his roommates bullying and threatening to hurt him. He asked to be moved to a different dorm, which the school took care of when he explained the situation. Thankfully, we had family in Dallas and he was able to go spend weekends with them to avoid any confrontations with the guys who were intent on bothering him. I prayed for his safety. I was also concerned for his spiritual welfare. Mike was a good Christian young man and certainly not a troublemaker. He and his cousins in Dallas would pray together when he'd go over, and that gave him the courage to endure the remaining days of the first summer session, because he had decided that SMU was not for him. That meant he had to be admitted to another university. But who would take him on such short notice? Where would he go? The Lord needed to open a new door. Something needed to happen quickly.

The need was urgent because Mike had not applied to any other university, and besides, applications were completed during the applicant's senior year, not a month before the starting fall semester. His chances of getting in anywhere were almost hopeless. I called several universities in the state only to get the response I knew so well. They were booked solid for the year, and even if he applied, he would only be considered for a start date the following year. He wanted me to go to Baylor and see if it would consider him, being that his brother was a rising junior there by that time. I refused to go and instead sent him and prayed for the Lord to intervene and open a door for Mike. He was desperate, and I was worried. What a dilemma.

After earnestly praying about the problem, I advised him to personally make a trip from Dallas to Waco to apply at Baylor University himself. He would later recall that I had also mentioned to him to not give up while there, regardless of the negatives encountered, and to continue knocking on doors until reaching the right one.

Mike made the trip upon my recommendation and reassurances. Needless to say, the first receptionist looked at him, when he mentioned the word *applying*, as if he was a total idiot. She informed him that they were booked solid for the next two years. Besides, the deadline for applications for the fall semester (beginning in five weeks) had passed nearly a year before. Of course Mike knew all this, but Mom had told him—assured him—that God would open a door for him and that he must not retract or retreat.

Dejected, as he walked away from the receptionist's desk, the words I'd told him sounded loudly in his ears. "When one door closes, God will open another. Don't give up. I'll be praying while you're knocking on doors, and God *will* open a door." When he heard my words, he went back to the receptionist and took the application and stated that he'd write the required letter and deliver both before the end of the day. The receptionist looked at him in disbelief, as if he were the most ignorant student on earth. Mike identified himself as a PK and explained that he couldn't give up or walk away, because his mother had taught him that if one door closed, God would surely open another and he was only obeying my instructions. After he submitted the paperwork that afternoon, he returned to Dallas, uncertain but hopeful.

Rey was at a pre-med conference in Chicago, Illinois. He was, however, fully aware of everything happening to Mike. Wanting to help somehow, he wrote letters, made phone calls, and talked to different people in administration, hoping his rapport as a member of Baylor Student Government could influence someone to at least take a glance at Mike's application and take note of its merit.

Two weeks later, my husband and I decided to visit Mike and spend the Fourth of July weekend with him. When we arrived in Waco, which is about an hour and a half drive from Dallas, I decided to stop by Baylor and ask about the status of Mike's application. After about a thirty-minute wait, I was finally allowed to talk to the lady in charge of applications, even though I had not set an appointment.

The first thing I saw on the lady's desk was an opened Bible. That was a good sign for me. I told her the reason for my unexpected visit and had just started to tell her about Mike when she just signaled to me to wait. She stood up, telling me she couldn't tell me anything without first getting his folder, and she added that she was sure no applications had been processed in the last couple of weeks. She said this as she was walking out of her office.

About two or three minutes later, she returned with a look of disbelief, saying, "This has got to be a miracle!" She was totally amazed at the approval for Mike's immediate acceptance. He could transfer to Baylor and even take courses in the second summer session. After repeating the same phrase a couple of times, she finally sat down and listened to me. I gave her the testimony and my reassuring words to Mike about the declared acceptance to Baylor.

Little did I know that God was working through me with the gift of faith. As shocked as she looked and acted, she asked if he wanted to start right away, and if so, all I had to do was post as little as fifty dollars and that would guarantee his spot. Talk about a miracle! We will never have words enough to express our gratitude to God or to explain the joy my husband and I felt as we drove off to Dallas. I was sure this miracle would be told time and again for generations to come.

Mike couldn't believe his ears when we shared the miracle that God had just performed. But while one minute he was overwhelmed with joy, the next minute he was worried, telling me he had just left the financial aid office at SMU and had been denied reimbursement for the summer classes we had paid for in advance. I wanted to shake him and make him see what I, by faith, had already seen. I simply reassured him that if God had taken care of the *big* issue, He would take care of the *littlest* details. We walked to the financial aid office once more, and there my Lord and Savior had an angel ready to assist us.

The gentleman that helped us claimed to be the manager. I explained what Mike had been told and denied just minutes before. Very calmly, he explained and guaranteed a full reimbursement. He told us that we'd be getting back 100 percent of our money and that we would've gotten only 80 percent if we had waited until after the Fourth of July. He was such a nice person, compared to the man that had spoken to Mike some minutes before. This gentleman's manners helped Mike feel comfortable and reassured. After signing some forms, we walked out of that office the happiest mom and son ever seen at SMU's campus, I'm sure.

We went to the car to share the second miracle with his father, and together we issued a prayer of thanksgiving and praises to the living God we serve.

The following day, Mike packed up his car and off we went to Waco just in time to watch the Fourth of July fireworks display. We stayed at a hotel that night and helped Mike move into his new dorm the next morning. He was finally at a different university where he would spend the following four years. There would be tough times at Baylor too, but Rey would soon be back from Chicago to welcome him, lend a hand, counsel, and pray with him.

Photograph taken at Mike's ring ceremony at Baylor University. Here Mike reaches over his brother to display his new Baylor ring while Rey displays his on his right hand.

CHAPTER 10

Moving Forward

All was well at church and now I could focus on my family, but more so on my retirement plans. The 2001–2002 school year was upon us and I was dead serious about retiring, so I went back to school in mid-August determined to retire by the end of the 2001 calendar year. A new principal had been assigned to our school, and in the first week of September, I informed him of my retirement plans for December, giving him ample time to process the needed paperwork and find a replacement for the remainder of the school year.

My new principal took it upon himself to prepare a retirement reception for me. He, not the school, would pay for all the expenses. He invited the entire school staff to the party. He even asked me to invite my family and friends—whoever I wanted to come celebrate with us. I figured that because everyone knew I was a pastor, this would be an ideal opportunity to share my testimony and give account of my walk with the Lord since age nine. What a farewell treat this would be.

December came along before I knew it. As if throwing the party wasn't enough, my principal also gave me a colorful, framed copy of the special invitation for my keepsakes. He seemed so proud of what he was doing for me, and I just kept praising the Lord.

Angels By The Roadside

The invitation prepared by my school principal, inviting faculty, staff, school district administrators, and guests to my retirement reception.

    The library was beautifully decorated and jam-packed with guests. I couldn't believe how many old teacher friends, ex-bosses, and people from the school district had shown up. I was somewhat nervous yet satisfied. After hearing so many good things from special guests and ex-principals of mine that had been asked to speak at the event, I was eventually handed the microphone to say a few words. I gave a short testimony of my walk with the Lord since age nine and of my call to the ministry in my teens. I also shared a few words of my thirty years as an elementary schoolteacher. Without going into details, I explained how for many of those years I overcame the challenge of keeping a career while coping with my husband's health. For thirteen consecutive years, I had taken my husband to a hospital in Houston for treatments. On numerous occasions, I had needed to be absent from school for one urgency or another. I praised God for the patience my superiors and fellow workers had had with me all along and thanked them for their prayers, support, and love.

That I had much on my plate was true. I was tending to my family and teaching in public school and in Bible school, all while tending to a church as senior pastor. When asked how I could handle it all, I would share my faith and explain how God's mercy and companionship helped me to endure and how His amazing grace would give me "wings to soar like an eagle." I share that in the highest peaks, He'd somehow renew my strength and prepare me to descend ready to face each day as it came. "Prayer," I would tell them, "prayer pulled me through." I ended my remarks at my retirement party with a prayer of exaltation to the King of Kings and Lord of Lords.

I will forever be thankful to the Lord for using my principal to prepare the stage for my public testimony and trust that the video recording of this grand reception will be treasured by my daughter and sons to share for generations to come as an example of how to seek every opportunity to bring God glory.

As a retiree, I could finally enjoy being a full-time pastor and a full-time wife and mom. Dina had been married for several years by now and had two wonderful children. I shifted my attention to my sons, who were in college and upon completion were going to move even farther away from us. "Lord, oh Lord," I prayed, "how I need your angels by my side now." I needed the same support that had assisted me for years to comfort me, but also to be there for my two now grown young men. Each was ready to go in a different direction while we, at home, prayed.

Rey graduated from Baylor University in 2002 and then came home and taught at the University of Texas at Brownsville for a year while he waited to be accepted to medical school. After a long wait, he was accepted to Ross University School of Medicine, a Caribbean medical school on the island of Dominica.

Both of my sons were going through tough times. Rey didn't like the island and was trying to adjust and stay the course for his career's sake. Mike was getting ready to graduate from Baylor when he suffered an almost fatal accident. He crashed into a tree while riding a four-wheeler just one month before graduation. I was able to bring him home to have surgery, giving him time to recuperate and drive back to Waco for the graduation ceremony.

Aided by a pair of crutches and the cheers of his fellow graduates, Mike was able to walk up the ramp to the platform and receive his degree. He yelled his lungs out with a cheer of victory that sparked a much greater cheer and applause from the audience. I'm sure he wished his brother had been there to hear it all, but unfortunately, he was still in Dominica finishing his final exams.

After completing his courses in Dominica, Rey transferred to Miami, Florida, where Mike joined him for several weeks. He'd been recovering after a second surgery on his ankle, and the trip would serve him good. Besides, Mike needed to be motivated to continue his studies and pursue a career, something he had put on hold due to the accident.

Mike must have been well motivated by his brother to explore his professional possibilities, because it wasn't long before Mike decided to go to Europe to continue his studies. I prayed that my guarding angels would follow him where he went. I had to let go and trust God for the end result. Mike left to Prague, Czech Republic, where few Christians existed and where, according to him, sin was pervasive and casual. If he was to come back a Christian, it would take a host of angels to help him in his daily walk in that faraway land. He would call often to tell us of his plans for the upcoming weekend trip to another European city or country. It was hard to keep up with Mike's whereabouts, so we made a colorful world map poster that read, "Where in the WORLD is Mike?" That poster hung in our dining room for many years.

Rey had met all his basic science requirements and decided to come home to study for Step 1 of the medical board exams before being assigned the location for his medical rotations here in the States. There was a lot of catching up to do since he hadn't been home for two long years. The year before starting medical school, Rey had obtained his private pilot license, accomplishing a childhood dream to someday fly airplanes. While in the Caribbean, he had taken up a new hobby and had become a certified scuba diver. By the grace of God, he was now a licensed private pilot, a certified scuba diver, and a medical student. Things were not all fun and games though. He spent many hours studying. After passing the USMLE Step 1 exam, he was assigned to begin rotations in Chicago.

Though he had to leave us again, his dad and I were happy knowing that upon completing his rotations he'd be graduating from medical school, his lifelong goal. Besides, Chicago was real close compared to the island of Dominica; we could go to Chicago any time we chose. With that, we committed our son to the Lord, who would protect and guide him through his new challenges and adventures in the hospital where he would be stationed for a while.

After nine months abroad, Mike not only returned with his faith intact but with an international degree in teaching English from a TOEFL program. We enjoyed him for only a month though, because at exactly the same time that Rey moved to Chicago to begin rotations, Mike moved to New York to begin a new job.

Although my sons were away, Dina and her family had settled in our own community. She kept in touch with her brothers and kept a watchful eye on us. As for angels, I'm a witness that they were always near.

CHAPTER 11

The Gates of Hell Break Loose

Mike's job in New York was appealing to him more because of the fringe benefits than the job itself. Such benefits included living in a bachelor pad with his best friend from Baylor, Stefan. That was short-lived though. After learning that Stefan had to relocate to a place where Mike could not follow, there was nothing really to keep Mike in New York. Rey Jr. offered for Mike to move to Chicago to live with him and get a job there. Mike took the offer, and before he knew it, he was working for a large, multinational investment firm as a certified financial adviser. The pay was good, but life in Chicago was a huge downfall for Mike. Spiritually, he was in the dumps. Only God's angelic hosts could draw him from the pit he had fallen into.

I got an army of prayer warriors to help me pray him out of the pit. I pleaded and called upon the Lord to send His angels—that had always been there for me—to do whatever it took to save my son. Mike tells how he cried to God for help and cried for spiritual restoration, but it seemed that the more he cried out, the more stuck he became in a dangerous cycle of infidelity to his Lord. Surely God could see him in that hour of desperation.

It took a miracle, but God did it again, I believe, for him and for me. God had promised in His Word that He wouldn't give us burdens we couldn't carry—and this one was too much for me to bear. The Angel of God, my Jesus, in His resurrected power (as He had done with His disciples), came onto the stage, and with one word, a sea of problems dissolved. The roaring, fierce tempest disappeared and the pitch-dark nights turned into the brightest days we'd ever seen. A new light shone in Mike's life. The Lord had answered our prayers, and Mike was restored spiritually and in every other sense of the word.

Rey was experiencing his own share of difficulties—all as a result of a seemingly perfect but actually weak and eventually unsustainable relationship. My sons and I knew we were facing a spiritual warfare. The gates of hell had unleashed their fury against us, the pastoral family. My husband, because of his illness, was kept in the blind of all the problems and spiritual battles we were facing. Dina shared our burden with every detail of the problems as they arose. All we could do was fast and pray and encourage each other. We knew in our hearts that God would eventually give us victory. Yes, the year 2007 was *the* nightmare year of our lives, but we declared that the bigger the battle, the greater the victory. With the turn of the New Year came new blessings, renewed strength, and triumph at last. Every demon, every evil force had been prayed off and cast back into its pit of torment. The angel of the Lord with His army of celestial warriors had descended to put a stop to the warfare. He fought all our battles. We had victory at last. Praise the Almighty.

In May 2008, Rey graduated from medical school. Several people from our church made the trip with us to his graduations in New York. I could feel God's presence in that auditorium. I could picture the Lord standing tall on the stage and smiling at those of us who had been hurting so much in the months leading up to graduation. The Lord was ready to show us His unwavering and everlasting love. Upon receiving his medical degree, many of us in attendance burst into tears of joy and gratitude.

All of us knew what Rey had gone through, and we were now contemplating God's victory in him—God had shown Himself faithful. Through it all, he remained strong in his unwavering faith and, as the

Patriarch Job in the Bible had, Rey had been put through the proverbial fire and had emerged like refined gold. He was able to prove to the world that greater was God that abided in him than he who rules the world. Rey's life was in the hands of the Creator and would eventually heal the wounds of the past and lead him to a much brighter and more blessed future. Praise God for young men like him who have consecrated their entire lives to the Lord, to His will, and to His service in the public arena. Matthew 16:18 reminds us, "The gates of hell shall not prevail …" That promise is prophetic and forward-looking and also applies in present-day, real-life adversities. It is a promise we claimed for ourselves, and God, who is always faithful to His Word, fulfilled His promise.

Attending Rey's medical school graduation helped Mike finally decide to pursue medicine. A month later, Mike left Chicago and moved to New York, where he had been accepted to attend St. John's University and begin his studies as a physician assistant. He seemed to fit right in place. He was finally free from the Chicago drag, enjoying student life once more.

Even before his graduation ceremony from medical school had taken place, Rey had already moved to Dayton, Ohio, and begun law school while pending medical residency training as a physician. Working on a JD would eventually pay off. There are few physicians in the world who are also lawyers. Why couldn't Rey Jr. be both? Rey González Jr., MD, JD. That, according to Dina, sounded very good. How she loved her brothers and was forever proud of their accomplishments. She had seen them suffer and sacrifice throughout their college years and could only hope that they would be great role models for her own kids, Michael Rey and Jason.

Who knows what the good Lord has for our only grandchildren thus far? I pray that God will give Dina and her husband, Mario, the courage He has given me. I pray that her faith will not waiver and that, as a mother, she too may always be there for her sons. I pray that she may stand tall, trusting God through the good times and the bad times.

I pray that she may learn from the gospel song that "the God on the mountains is the God of the valleys; the God of the good times is the God of the bad times; and the God of the day is still the God in the night."

CHAPTER 12

Angels Will Welcome Me Home

Wherever the Lord leads me, I will follow. One day, He will lead me to my eternal home. In the meantime, I will continue spreading the gospel and telling others of my very best friend, Jesus Christ. I also want to share the joy it has been for me to have such a wonder family, bound as one by the power of the Holy Spirit. We suffered and cried together, but we also rejoiced and laughed together. And rejoice we did—especially when the good Lord added a new member to our family who fit in just right.

In 2013, Mike married a beautiful, kind, caring, and tender young lady named Kim. The Almighty, in His divine plans, had her there at St. John's University in the same Physician Assistant School in New York just for him. The seal showing it was God's doing was when Kim accepted Christ into her heart and fell in love with my Jesus. Today, they are not only very successful physician assistants but also a happy Christian couple serving God and the church where they attend. Mike can't believe that he, too, is in the medical field, and all because of the impact Rey's medical school graduation ceremony had on him that day, outside Madison Square Garden in New York City.

Even though his heart is still in medicine, after finishing law school, Rey was admitted to the Texas Bar and has been practicing law in a small but lucrative private practice. God works in mysterious ways, and His plans are far better than ours.

As for me, in February 2015, I finally accomplished something I had impulsively begun to desire when I was seventeen years old—just because an old boyfriend had given me a "Baylor" watch. I, too, became an alumna of Baylor University—an official alumna by choice, that is. I received a certificate and everything.

An official Alumna by Choice from Baylor University, February 28, 2015

Today, I am still pastoring Ebenezer and count it a privilege to introduce new converts to my wonderful friend, Jesus. Choosing to overlook the hard times, focusing on the good, I can honestly declare, "What a great life!"

I have grown old—just turned seventy-one—and it has been more than sixty years since my very first experience with God when I became a Christian at age nine. And I love my God, my family, and my church better every day. What a privilege it has been to have served God all my life and to have had the opportunity to introduce my family to Him too. I couldn't ask for more.

I don't know just how many more years the good Lord will give me or my husband, but I do know one thing, and that is that we intend to serve Him and live for Him the rest of our days. Angels will always be a part of our lives; I trust they will be present in our dying moments to usher us to God's great welcome-home reception.

I know the day will come when, as painful as it may be, my family will close my eyes forever with a spirit of satisfaction. I only hope that the pain of temporary separation will be overshadowed by the joy to see, by faith, a host of angels by my bedside ready to transport me home. May God comfort them by reminding them, even in their days of mourning, that I strongly believed I'd be greeted by a multitude of celestial beings welcoming the person they had assisted many a time while journeying on Earth. May they be comforted knowing that I will see my *Angels by the Roadside*, recognizing them and remembering their specific interventions on my behalf. May they know that I will finally be with the angel of the Lord, my Jesus, my Lord and Savior - and with my Mom!

May my loved ones enjoy peace and retain the faith that will cause them to serve God until we meet again. Now, that's what you call a bountiful life: a beautiful relationship and a marvelous future to enjoy for an eternity!

I pray this book has inspired you to share your very own experiences in the Lord, whether big or small. Remember that every Christian is given the opportunity to walk with God and individually experience His love, His power, and His protection. Angels will be there for you too, as they will have been for me throughout my life.

My family in 2014. From left to right, standing: Mario, Dina, me, Mike, Kim, Michael Rey, Jason, and Rey Jr. Sitting: Reynaldo (Rey Sr.)

www.ingramcontent.com/pod-product-compliance
Ingram Content Group UK Ltd.
Pitfield, Milton Keynes, MK11 3LW, UK
UKHW041958230426
12048UKWH00008B/398